CW00553612

FROM
MALTA
TO EAST
LONDON

Carmelo Micallef

Grosvenor House
Publishing Limited

The right of Carmelo Micallef to be identified as the author of this
work has been asserted in accordance with Section 78
of the Copyright, Designs and Patents Act 1988

The book cover is copyright to Carmelo Micallef

This book is published by
Grosvenor House Publishing Ltd
Link House
140 The Broadway, Tolworth, Surrey, KT6 7HT.
www.grosvenorhousepublishing.co.uk

A CIP record for this book
is available from the British Library

ISBN 978-1-83975-831-7

PREFACE

The story you are about to read is nothing but a true one, if anything it is less than what happened because it happened so long ago. All the hunger, the bullying, the war, being brought up without a father during World War Two, being the underdog, being humiliated by bigger boys, the tribalism, the racism when in England, and facing all the challenges from a very early age till I was 81 when everybody thought I was mad to do the challenge I was about to take on.

The challenges during my early days were forced on me, but as I grew up, they became a way of life, and I loved and looked forward to every one of them as it happened. I needed them for inspiration to do things my way, like writing this book at 85 years old because I had never written two lines in my life before.

Because of my early humble life, I never grew up with big ambitions, but with a lot of confidence in myself – from the toys I made at a young age, through playing football, overseeing a very important project at 18 years old, and through my working life where I always looked for new adventures. And although I am not going to say I was the best, other people said it instead, many times, and my superiors had full confidence in me.

CHAPTER 1

In this chapter, I start the story of my life, which began on 25 November 1934. I was born into a family of five; my mother, father, two sisters and two brothers. My story begins on 15 August 1938, which makes me four years old, and I want you to remember these dates, especially the 15th of August and my date of birth, because what I am going to say and tell you about myself is going to be impossible for you to believe. When I tell you something that I have done, I would like you to refer all the time to the date I was born. It might sound a bit exaggerated, but I would like you to remember that it was a different time when it happened; we were going through a different time to today.

The 15th of August 1938 was the date that changed my life and the life of my whole family, especially my poor mother. The day started early afternoon; my father had just returned from Gozo, where he went with his brother for the feast of Santa Maria. Because it's a big feast in Malta and Gozo and in the morning they have horse racing and also a big agricultural show, my father went to see the races, and when they came back he wanted to have a little sleep, but I remember we were playing and making a lot of noise so we woke him up, and with that, he decided to go and have a cup of coffee with his brother in Mensija, the local bar. I want you to remember the name of the bar because I will mention it later.

The next thing I remember, we all went to a little square by Mensija Bar where there was a big crowd gathered. All I remember is a big gathering and a lot of women crying. I was picked up by one of my neighbours, and because I was higher, I could see all of the scene. I didn't have any idea what happened or what was happening. I don't know today whether I realised that my father and his brother were shot, and all I remember is a lot of people crying, a lot of confusion, and my neighbour hugging me and comforting me.

I do not remember anything more till the middle of the night when there was a knock on the door, and my mother went to open it and came back crying, and that was the last thing I knew of my father. However, I want to tell you what happened with my father and his brother; they were shot, and it ruined my life and the lives of all the family forever.

My uncle lived with his father and his sister Anne, and my uncle sold a hunting dog to this Gozo man. I will carry on with this story at a later time.

The house I grew up in

Before I move on, I will tell you a bit about my parents. Both their families were well to do, especially on my mother's side. As I learned through the years, my mother's father owned 30 pieces of land and two farmhouses in Pebbly Beach and one beautiful house in a prime position in Tal Gharghur. It had two yards and about three bedrooms and it also had a garden, and in those days they used to call it Jardina, which is a French word for garden. They had orange trees and other fruit trees, and the interesting thing was when the two of them went to pick up the bread, they used to sleep there and get the bread early next morning and take the bread to the farmhouse where they lived. It lasted for a whole week, and there was no refrigeration so I don't know how they used to manage.

That's why I said earlier to always remember the times we are talking about. They also used to sleep some in one farmhouse and some in another farmhouse; the main farmhouse was in the centre of Pebble Beach. The place consisted of four farmhouses and a villa, and a big house and the Church of San Gwann. I will come back to this area at a later stage when I will say what this area meant to me and the whole of my mother's family.

On my father's side of the family, my grandad owned six houses and a big area of land adjoining one of the houses where he lived. He was a farmer and also, from what I hear, a businessman. One of the businesses used to export potatoes, and in my time, I remember they used to export them in wooden barrels. Legend has it that one of my uncles was put in a barrel, and the barrel was loaded on a ship and eventually ended up in New York. I don't know if it's true or not, but the fact is that he did end up in New York. I have never talked to him, and my mother was never given his address to write to him. I will probably come to it when I come to talk about my terrible uncles and aunts from my father's side.

I will tell you about my father, and I will continue with my personal story. It was one September day in 1939, about seven in the morning; I was going with my older brother Joseph and my sister Marie – she was the oldest at 10 years old. We were not far away when the world exploded. I did not know what was happening; we hugged each other, then as a four-year-old, I tried to see what was happening.

First, a lot of people were coming out of their houses, not knowing where to run to. Then, just a few metres away, a man was putting the harness and cart on a horse when his mother came out of the house screaming and carrying a cross and telling the man to put the horse back in the house because the war had started. As you can imagine, in the confusion I was in, to see such a scene, I don't remember anything else; it was something like a vision after that.

CHAPTER 2

THE WAR YEARS

At the beginning of the war, we used to go to a cave to shelter from the bombs. This was situated in a place called Olliqa Valley, which today is a nature reserve, it was about half a mile from home. Another cave that we used as a shelter belonged to Mensija Bar. One of the sons was George, a friend of mine, and one day we were in this cave, which was used as a well before the war, and one of us landed against one of the walls, and it sounded hollow. So we broke a hole in the wall and found a little niche, and we found a skeleton of a young child. Again, my story ends here because I don't know what happened after that. This is time to reflect about when I was born, my stories, when my father was killed, when the war started, and the skeleton. I happened to find when writing this book that it all appeared like a vision, and then it came to a sudden stop.

I don't know what age I was when the cave episode happened because soon after the war started and the government started digging shelters. I will leave it to your imagination.

They dug a shelter. One of the entrances was next to my grandad's house. I remember this vividly because when my grandfather died, again there was a vision. I Remember when he was taken to the cemetery in a horse-driven hearse, and next to the house there was this big tower of stones that they dug from the shelter, so the hearse had to manoeuvre around it. My vision was of the scene of my road and the shelter; the other entrance was about 30 metres away on the other side of the road.

The hardship

When the siren sounded, everybody ran to the shelter with the mothers shouting at the children to hurry up, including my mother. Speaking for myself, I didn't like the shelters. When going into the shelters, you went down about four flights of stairs; it also had two entrances. The shelters had one big room, and the people who could afford it dug their own room, which made us poor people very envious because they put their own bits and pieces in and what they used for mattresses was filled with straw. Later, I should tell you about one of my mischiefs.

As I remember, in the early days, a lot of people had what they called scabies caused by hunger and fright from the bombs. I remember the worst person to get this disease was a woman who lived next door to us who come from Zebbug. They had two daughters, Rose and Pola, and lots of animals and rats; they also had a farm not far from where we lived where they used to keep milk cows. The woman had to be carried from home down the shelter, and she was crying, and that's all I remember about that. We all had a bit of this scabies, some worse than others; we weren't too bad. Myself, I had some between the fingers of my hands.

We lived in San Gwann, which is located on a bit of a hill about six miles to the sea to the north. The planes from Sicily and Germany approached Malta from the north, and the first fort the planes encountered was Madliena on the left of us, then past St. Julian's. On the hill was a fort called Ta Gorney, then the plane went over our heads, and then the show started because to the south of us there was a fort called Tal Qroqq where the university and Mater Dei Hospital are. Also, we could see the harbours and Valletta and the dockyards and Luqa and Hal Far airports, so as you can imagine, I had a front seat to a big show.

It used to start with the sound of the sirens, and as we ran to the shelters, we could see the planes coming towards us from a distance, approaching from the north. I do mean the planes because there were between

40 to 60 in a square formation, shining in the sun, loaded with bombs, heading towards the ports and the airports, and I was under their route. Tal Qroqq Fort was about half a mile from me, so as soon as the planes flew past me, the fort used to open the guns, firing at the planes. What a sight to see the flames coming out of the cannons and looking forward to planes being shot and the noise they made when they were coming down. Sometimes the pilot would come down by parachute, and as I followed him falling, I could see the army and Maltese men carrying shotguns, running to where the pilot was going to land to make sure he would not escape the Maltese. Men tried to get the parachute because the women liked the material.

The planes carried on bombing the harbour and the airport, and I could also see what was going on around the airport: total confusion, with planes trying to take off to find the Italian aircraft, bombs falling. I could see the dust going up when the bombs hit the ground and, of course, the cannons shooting and more planes coming down.

We used to have air raids that lasted five to ten hours, and every day and night, and among this confusion, life had to carry on. At the start of the war, the Italian planes used to bomb Malta and they used to stay very high, drop the bombs and go home. Of course, we used to think they were cowards, but as I learned later, they were forced into the war and didn't like what they were doing. One morning, I was in a field we called Ta Grezju as we heard the silence or the noise of planes. We knew what was coming, so my mother rushed me into this small room, which would fall with a big gust of wind, never mind a bomb. As the planes passed us, we came out of the room to watch the show, and as they approached the harbour they started to dive and dive until they were exceptionally low. Before they dropped the bombs, my mother commented that these planes were different; that was when the German planes came to Malta – in 1941. Which means I was seven years old.

The room we used in Swieqi Field

Continuing with the theme of the war, I will start with suffering. As I mentioned before, people suffered through the hardship – lack of food, no sleep because of air raids, and other stresses. Due to my mother's energy and determination, none of us were very affected by hunger because people were eating what they thought was edible. It was tough; some people were eating prickly pear leaves, the saying goes that there was not a cat alive in Malta after the war; that was the state the people of Malta had gone through.

Back to me and my family. My mother without a husband, and with five children to feed received no help from the authorities, whether it was the government or the British Army. We had no food apart from about half a litre of soup for five of us, which came from the Victory Kitchen.

Today is Thursday 14 May 2020, and because of the virus and the lockdown, people are comparing today's hardship with the war. I can tell people that there is no comparison because as a seven-year-old starving child, I don't think I can compare what we ate apart from the soup. As I said before, my mother's family were farmers, and my grandad and two uncles were the people from heaven because they saved our lives by giving us all the farm produce. Because everything was watched by the army and the Maltese police, one of my uncles, Bertu, brought the products from their fields covered by hay.

He also made sure that we had a supply of wheat, and that was the main sort of food my mother used to feed us. She used an old mill to turn it into powder; it used to take ages and sometimes my older sister Marie used to help her. My mother used to make soup with it, I don't know how it tasted, but when you waited by the wardrobe because that was the only lockable cupboard in the house for hours for one slice of bread, then you eat everything that is in front of you. I remember sitting in one of the rooms where my mother used to keep animal food, sitting on bales of straw or a sack filled with something, eating mostly Maltese carob, which was just a skin. I don't know what else we used to eat.

I know we used to spend a lot of time in that room. We also had a big bag of sugar hidden under the straw, which my mother's sister Catherine gave her. Imagine if her husband was caught by the army when he brought it to us because he worked for the forces, of course.

We also worked two fields, one in Swieqi and one in Ta Grezju, so we also got some products from them when it wasn't pinched. As you might realise, because I mentioned the generosity towards us that came from my mother's side, I will expand on it later. I will explain the difference between the two families. Carrying on, at the age of seven, apart from the bombing and the hardship, we were going through life as best we could. For me, life was full of different things, some I am proud of and some I regret what I have done, and some

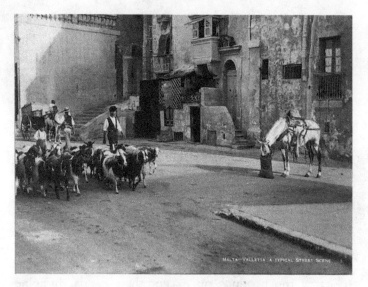

Taking goats to Sliema at seven years old

I am ashamed of the grief I caused, especially to my mother and some of the neighbours.

My Mother

I think it is time to tell you something about my mother; everybody should think highly of their mother, so I am not going to say anything, and I will leave it to your imagination.

She was born at the beginning of the century into a family of 9, seven girls and two boys. The girls' names, I thought, were very nice: Catherine, Ganina, Carmen, Guzeppa, Celeste, Marjanna, Grezja. The older boy was called Bertu, short for Robert, and the younger was Michael. As a child, she had to get involved, helping with whatever she was able to do, and it was hard work. She was loved by her parents, so she wasn't mistreated as badly as I hear that at that time in England some children were, who were used to work in the mines and other terrible places. The family worked in the fields from dawn to dusk. Besides doing all that, I learned lately that her mother took one of the girls, sometimes it was my mother, to sell the crops.

They used to take produce to sell in Sliema and Valletta market; nothing to it, except they had nothing to carry the produce on except their heads. Imagine carrying a basketful of fruit on your head and walking a distance of seven to eight miles!

That was only to Sliema; when it was Valletta day, they walked to Sliema to catch the ferry to Valletta and walked up the hill to the market to sell the produce. I was only told a few months ago that her father gave her a very good sum of money that paid for all the furniture and a horse and cart because my father shared the horse with his brother before that.

I will go back to the age of seven and continue with my mother. She used to work two fields. One in Swieqi and one we called Ta Grezju, which was less than a mile

My Mother

away from home. Swieqi was about a mile and a half away, and we had to carry as much as we could of the produce and also food for the animals, which was mostly uphill hard work. The two fields came to about 10 acres. When the fields needed ploughing, my mother paid somebody with a horse to do it; she used to get help paying, of course, with other work that needed the use of a horse, such as sowing of potatoes.

They used to get the seed potatoes from Scotland, and when planting day arrived, it started about three or four in the morning. The neighbour and his wife used came to help; they cut the potatoes into small pieces with a growing eye in each piece. Of course, I was fast asleep except when I was woken up by a ghost, which I will mention later in my ghost stories. When they finished cutting the potatoes, we all went to the fields to sow them. The horse opened the farrow with a plough, and because the horse was fast, we used to share the length of the farrow. We would hang a bag on our neck full of potatoes, walk in the farrow and drop one every foot and step on it. I remember doing it but I don't know at what age I started, although I know I was young. So as you can see, that was hard work and my mother had the task of getting the children to do it.

I do not know when she started making shirts for young boys in the village, and soon she was making shirts for older boys. I do not know how she managed to do it because she never had anybody to teach her. I know that on British Empire Day, the school had to do some performance in the main football stadium and we had to wear white shirts and black shorts. I remember one of the neighbours gave her a pair of black trousers and she made me a pair of shorts. I do not know if she made the shirt, and I don't know where she got the shoes from because all I used to wear was sandals. Anyway, we had to do this drill for which we practised for months. Soon after that, when the war finished and life began to improve, my brother Joseph lost his sight in both eyes; it must have been a big shock for my mother. Life went on with my mother coping as best as she could, and it was not many years later that my brother was taken to a home; I remember to this day my uncle Gamri carrying him out of the door with my mother crying.

When Marie became a teenager, she got a job as a housemaid in Sliema as a lot of girls did, and as she grew up, the boys started taking an interest in her. Another disaster for my mother as Marie started losing her sight until she lost the sight in both eyes. By this time, I must have been about 12 years old. You can't imagine how this could happen to two healthy youngsters; some said that Joe hit his head on a tree trunk when he was cutting carob. I do not know what caused it to happen; even when I spoke to my sister

Rose I did not learn anything even though she was a nurse. Anyway, the mystery continued; lots of people thought it must be some sort of curse until somebody suggested to my mother to speak to a woman in Birkirkara, which was the next village, and she must have said that she could help identify the person who placed the curse if it was true. The woman asked my mother to get something from everybody, as many people as possible, and it was easy for my mother to do that because of the sewing she used to do.

The woman arrived and she told my mother what she needed, so my mother had the kenur (it was a stone cut to use for cooking with wood) in the yard where we keep the animals, they started the fire and on top of it the woman put a big frying pan.

She put all the pieces of clothes in the frying pan and started chanting something until all the pieces of clothes burnt except for one.

I suppose it was sort of black magic and, according to the woman, that cloth belonged to the person who placed the curse. Right away, my mother identified the man the cloth belonged to.

And as it happens, she remembered when we were coming from the field together and the man had said, 'Look at Grace, she soon will have grown children to help her,' or something like that, some time passsed. Soon after, the man became terribly ill and spent a long time in bed, and to add to his disaster, one day, all his gold and his possessions were stolen. I do not know what happened to him after that. Seeing it all as a child was strange.

The next hard time for us, especially for my mother, started when I was 14 years old. I had just left school and it was time for my father's family to share my grandad's estate. There was Gamri, Manwel, Janna, Anny, and Carmel, who was in New York, and of course there was us children. Because in Malta the law is different to England, when my father died, everything he had belonged to the children not the wife, and that was when the trouble started. Somebody had to have Power of Attorney to act on our behalf, which my mother thought was her right to be that person. But my uncles did not like the idea in case she got married again and we ended up with nothing. The family were having arguments with my mother, and it began to get nasty. Luckily for my mother, she had a very good lawyer so at least she had somebody to help her; he was also a member of parliament, so with his help, my mother got the Power of Attorney. But to the others, things were not going fast enough, so they kept hassling my mother instead of giving her some help with her problems. As a child, I had to watch this going on and felt helpless, and it only increased the hate I felt against them.

One day, my mother was working in our field in Swieqi when the three of them – Gamri, Manwel, and

Wenzu, who was married to Ganna – went to have a go at her. She told us how angry they were and how scared she was when the big men, especially Gamri, started shouting madly at her, so she ran until she got home. It was then that I decided to do something about it the next time. Soon after that, the family had a meeting coming up, and I thought it was my opportunity to do something to repay my uncles for the way they treated my mother. I will leave that to later because it will not make any sense until you know me better.

My parents

Anyway, the saga continued. Tony employed an architect to divide the properties; he split one house into two properties, and because some were worth more than others, the better ones had to pay money and that became one share, and some money was allocated to the smallest property.

The raffle was done and our share was the smallest property, and the sum of £60 was included with the house. Again, my uncles accused my mother and her lawyer of including that £60 themselves. They took every opportunity to have a go at my mother, but my mother must have been a very strong-willed person and proved that the money was included by the architect. As I said before, our share was half the house that was split into two; the other went to Carmel who was in America, so my mother asked my uncles for his address but they refused. We were allowed to stay where we lived until my mother extended the property we were going to move into. My mother could not wait to move because in the house we had problems with a ghost – again, I will come to it later.

My mother opened the first shop in San Gwann, she sold some clothes and household goods. When the shop started to do well, she got rid of the fields. John and I were not interested in working the fields, and by now we were both working. How my mother managed the shop is a mystery because she never learned to read and write, but somehow, she put on paper things that she needed to remember, objects such as stock and things she sold on the never.

In San Gwann near the shop they built a lot of flats for English families and they were good customers; she managed to converse with them as well. By this time, she'd become well known in San Gwann because it saved people going miles to buy something like a broom. Although by now she was 72, and that's when the money changed to metric, the shopkeepers went to be taught how it worked. You'd think that would be hard work for her, but no, she finished top of the class. After some time, she suffered with one of her knees and it was time to close the shop. She lived till the age of 92, and in all that time she was never ill except when she got very old. Sometimes, she asked to see the doctor because she did not feel well; the doctor came to examine her and found nothing was wrong with her and she got out of bed when the doctor went. All she wanted was a bit of reassurance. That was one hard life.

CHAPTER 3

THE WAR YEARS

Because a lot was happening in my life, I will tell different stories about different things such as the war years, my school years, and after the war, and my working life, which started when I was about seven or younger.

The war years informed the rest of my life. The bullying taught me that there was never anybody to help me, so I had to do things the best way I could my way.

While the bombs were raining all over Malta, life went on the best it could, so I will start with the bullying. All the time when I was young, Mensija Bar and the square in front of it was always a meeting place where all the boys and men used to meet. The men used to go for a drink and the teenagers did their own thing, like playing games. Some Maltese games included playing marbles; I remember one of my cousins had a bucketful. I did not have any because I never had any money.

Sometimes they used to look for something else to entertain themselves with; this is where I come in. To get to the Mensija, I had to come out of my street, and I was in the area. On the corner on the right lived Joe, my age but a lot bigger than me, and as I came out of my street on the left about three doors away lived Tony. When the bigger boys felt like having a laugh, they'd get one of them to wet his finger with spit and put it on my nose, and that's how the fight started. Joe used to fight a normal fight and I used to beat him, but Tony was a different cup of tea; he always picked up a stone to fight with and the older boys did nothing about it, so I had to fight him and beat him. That went on for a long while until they gave up. By this time, I had learned my fighting skills, and when the fighting finished, it was time to wonder what made me go there to face the fighting and the jeering from the big boys because I was the underdog without anybody to support me.

I do not know what made me do it, but I suppose I learned at that young age if something had to be done, you just had to do it.

In front of our house lived George. He used to start on my brother and me, although he did mix with other children. He used to call us all sorts of names and run in

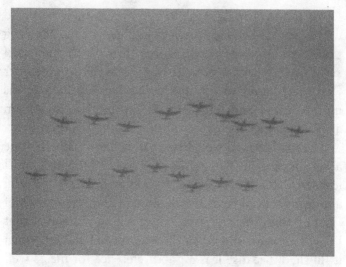

Small fleet of attacking German planes

the house, but I promised John that I would get him one day, so I told John to tell me if George strayed away from the house. As it happens, one day John told me that George was near the Borg man, a big man who lived a few doors down the road, so I ran after George and caught him by a load of stinging nettles. Anyway, I started to fight him with John telling me to hit him. Mr Borg tried to separate us, but this time I pushed George in the stinging nettles. He tried to lift me off George, but somehow he could not separate us.

As John was telling me to carry on, somehow, I held on to George between my legs and every time Mr Borg pulled me up, I dragged George through the nettles. I suppose my legs were hurting as well; I remember George running to his mother crying. Of course, his mother came and had a go at my mother, and I am afraid that was one of the types of things to come.

George behaved well after that; he eventually became a very nice man. George learned about bullying, and I learned a bit more about wrestling. Before I tell you about my school years, I will tell you about the mischief I got up to during the war. I want you to remember that I was four years old when the war started and ten when it finished, because it is a good reference for me as well as I cannot believe that I was a child of that age doing the things I did.

About half a mile from where I lived, the army had a big ammunition dump which contained petrol as well, and across the road, the army had a small place where they put used cartridge shells. I decided to go and pinch some of these shells, so I found some wood and wheels from an old pram and made a cart; as I remember, it was about a metre and a half long and seven fifty wide. So the time came to go and take some of these shells. I do not think the army had any security where they were, so I went and picked some and took them home. My mother did not let me take them in; I pleaded with her and offered to take them to Treszu field where we had a small well and put them in it, but she would not let me do that either. Listening to all this was my next-door neighbour, the Gozo woman, and she offered to take them, so I had no choice but to give them to her. Her daughter Rose, who was my age, offered to come with me next time I went, and her mother agreed with her. So next time we went to get some shells, when we were there, we heard two bikes coming so we hid in a carob tree trunk, but we could not hide the cart. Anyway, I could hear them walking with their big boots. One said, 'They are here because their cart is still here,' and as you can imagine, we were terrified.

As there were no big trees that you could hide in, I believe they wondered what they would do with two young children when Hitler was keeping them fully occupied. They left, and we loaded the cart. When I got home, I told my mother I would not go again if she let me take some in, so for some reason I took three in, which are still in my mother's house today. I hope one day I will bring one or two to England. Just after the war, they were in demand and worth a lot of money, so the Gozo woman did well, and all I had was the adventure.

Anyway, that didn't stop me, and Rose and I kept going and gave the shells to her mother, and she was very pleased with them. I was always at their house and at their farm with Rose; I will come to Rose later. Coming to the big ammunition dump, I remember only one instance. I do not know how I got in, but I was past the guard and was among the petrol tins; they used two types of tin, one about four hundred by one hundred and five by six hundred – they were used on Land Rovers; if you go to a fair and see old Land Rovers, look for the tins at the back. The other tins were square and of thinner tin. As I was hiding, a Maltese man walked past me. He had a hessian sack behind his back and he was walking fast. I could hear some liquid making a noise. As he got about 20 metres from me, a guard appeared from the right and shouted, Stop or I shoot!' With that, the man started running, so the guard fired a shot in the air. The man dropped the sack and ran, I think he had petrol in the tin, and that's the only thing I remember.

By the time the adventure of the shells finished because my mother decided to break my cart into hundred pieces, I became very friendly with Rose and her family. As I said before, they had all kinds of animals at home and on the farm, and I used to spend a lot of time with Rose. One day that we looked forward to was Sunday as her father used to set the rat traps in the farm on a Saturday because they had a lot of rats, and the next morning the traps used to be full of rats. In the field outside, they had a square room but without a roof where the farmers stored water – if you go to Malta, you see them in the fields. The room was empty of water, but in the bottom of the room they had somewhere where the rats could hide. Rose's father's friend had two fox terrier dogs, so on Sunday he used to bring the dogs to the farm; he put the dogs in the room with the rats and the hunt started. It was good to see the dogs hunting and exciting to see the dogs bite the rat and just throw it away when the rat was dead. So the show did not last long, but it was good to watch and enjoy myself and forget about the bombs and the hunger.

One day Rose told me she was going to Gozo with her family to her cousin's wedding, and after the wedding Rose stayed with her cousin for a few days. When she came back, she told me that she had watched her cousin and her husband in bed and she thought her cousin liked it and she would like to do the same. So, she explained to me how things happened and we decided to try it, but the question was where we would hide to do it. In a field on the way to their farm there was a small room, built only with stone and very small, about one and a half foot square, big enough for two small children anyway; we found some cardboard boxes, and everything went well.

Another place was behind San Gwann Church where there was a dip in the ground, and we made another layer in it. All this was happening when I was seven, remember, because one day we were behind the church, and when we came out we met my mother. She asked me where I was because I needed to go to confession because next day I was going to have my first holy communion, and that's the age we used to have it.

Goodness knows what I confessed, anyway I got blessed and I was alright for the morning holy communion.

Things went on, and I think Rose's mother knew that we were always together because I heard her say to my aunt how well we get on and how we always came out from the same dark place.

After a while, Rose's family moved away to a new house and a farm together. It was not far away, but I only remember going to their farm once because I saw something to remember, one of the farmers nearby brought a cow to be mated with Rose's father's bull. The bull was in a room on his own tied to his manger with a chain through his nose ring; the chain went through two rings on either side of the bull and tied on each end. They took the cow into the room near the bull and two men released the chains slowly until the bull could do his bit. When the bull finished, they pulled the chains and tied them again. I explain what happened because when I see young children holding bulls in England, I wonder why, although we always believed that male animals such as a horse or a donkey born in Malta were very lively. I knew one of these donkeys very well; it was uncontrollable. One day the owner raced it with another horse in a private race. A lot of men put lots of money on the race when it was organised, and because it was illegal it started at five in the morning. The race started and the donkey was in front, one horse tried to hold the donkey back, so the donkey's owner got two handguns out and fired two shots in the air and pointed the guns at the intruder, who very promptly pulled his horse out of the way and he went on to win the race.

Going back to Rose, I do not remember going to her house or the farm or see her again, although I used to pass her house every time I went to the field in Swieqi, and I had friends that lived two doors from her. I do not remember their names, I think their surname was Grima, the family moved to San Gwann to get away from Sliema and the bombs and I think the father was a Lawyer. What I remember about them was that we used to play soldiers, they lived near the cart ruts, and that's where we played. There were some holes in the rocks, and in two of the holes we made a sort of dugout and covered them with green camouflage. The reason I remember all this was because they had the idea to connect the two dugouts together, and we found two tins, put a hole in the bottom of the tins, put a string through the holes, and put one tin in each of the dugouts, which were about 20 to 30 metres apart, and we could talk to each other. I don't know where they got the idea from but it worked. Talk about playing soldiers! Another time, we were marching in line down towards San Gwann Church, and when we got in front of the church, I found a half-pound note, which was worth about a hundred of today's money. And because the money was different then, considering all I used to get was five to six pence as a Christmas present, how

Cart ruts where I played soldiers

San Gwann Church

happy I was. Unfortunately, it did not last long. A man pushing a bike on the other side of the road crossed over to me and told me that it was his. He took the money and he went up the road again. I found no one to help me and I ran to tell my mother, and I can imagine how my mother felt because probably that would have bought food for a week or more. We are still during the war, with bombs falling day and night. I am going to tell you two stories which today do not make good reading, but I would like you to remember that I was used as an exhibition myself when I was made to fight with the two boys, and I am not trying to tell you that two wrongs make a right, but I am trying to tell you the type of life I lived.

By this time, I had made friends with Tony, who became a very naughty boy, so we always looked for some sort of adventure. We got hold of some unfired cartridges and we took the bullet top off, and instead of powder, we found something that looked like spaghetti but a bit thinner. We emptied a few cartridges and decided to make some sort of a bomb. We found a tin of corned beef, put some of what we called 'cordy' in it, closed it and left some cordy sticking out and lit it, and it went about two metres high and 20 to 30 metres away. We then looked for something more interesting to do. I do not know where we found a sparrow, but we decided to tie the sparrow to the bomb and light it; the bomb went up and travelled some distance, then the string must have burned and the sparrow flew away as fast as it could.

In winter, we used to go where the cart ruts were and find frogs because the holes that we used as dugouts used to fill with water. So what would you do when you got one or two big frogs? So me or Tony came up with the idea to put a straw up the frog's bum and try to blow it up, and unfortunately for the frog, we succeeded. When we thought the frog was big enough, we put it on the ground and the frog flew away like the cordy bomb. The frog landed and hopped away with the straw still in his bum; that was the first of the things I did that I am not proud of.

Another thing I was involved in with Tony was when a woman across the road had an argument with my mother, so I wanted to do something in revenge. I suggested to Tony that I was thinking of burning the mattress they had in their private room in the shelter. Of course, being the type of a boy he was, he was all for it, so down we went when nobody was around and burned their mattresses. Unfortunately, the woman found out that I did it, so although the mattress was only filled with straw, my poor mother had to pay for the mattress, I am sorry to say. This was the second time of the many times to come that my mother had to cope with the problems that I would cause. One day I found a handgun that my father must have had, and there were also some bullets with it, so I took it to Ta Grezju field to try it, and although my aim was not very good, I enjoyed it. Next time I saw Tony, I told him about the gun and that I did not have a lot of bullets. He told me that he had enough bullets for the two of us and that he had a gun as well; he showed me a box full of bullets, so we decided to go and do some shooting. When I tried the bullets in my gun, they were a bit thinner, and I do not know how we did it, but we found a bit of tin wire, cut it to size and wrapped it around the groove at the bottom of the bullet. I put it in my gun and tried it and it fired OK; how dangerous that must have been I don't know. I remember we used to go to long life valley; we had a target one side of the valley and we shot from the other side, and don't ask me about our aim. The funny thing was, nobody ever told us off. By this time, you'd think that Tony was my best friend. I don't think the fighting that went on between us ever went away but stayed with us for the rest of our lives. Even when we went to England together, there was always a certain distance between us, but when we were young, we suited each other. He was well known for his daredevil acts till we left for England, while I settled down when I started proper work.

My best friend was a boy called Julian, he was my age and a very nice person, a bit different from Tony, he had a nice manner about him. Because he was bigger than me, he used to try to wrestle me, but he did not have my experience so he did not win, and one day I thought I would knocked his teeth out. I never forgot it; it happened not far from Mensija Bar. He came to get hold of me, and I sort of flung him to the side of me, and as he flew away, somehow his knee hit his face, and when his hand went to his face, I expected the worst, but that did not stop him. While I was writing this book, the thought came to mind that it was some sort of affection; it was nothing else.

One day a group of us were messing about. Tony was there, and Julian and a few other boys, and Tony got the gun out. The gun went off and Julian shouted 'ouch' and touched his side. We all rushed to see what happened, and we saw the shirt was burned and his side was also burned. A very narrow escape but that did not stop me from being friendly with the gun. When we ran out of bullets, we used to go to a house in Birkirkara and buy bullets. Can you imagine that today – a child buying bullets? I will come to the gun later.

The School Days

It must have been very important for my mother for me to be educated. I remember her taking me to the nurses in Birkirkara, which was about a mile and a half from home. All I remember is going for an interview; I do not remember going for lessons.

I don't remember starting school because, as I said before, the past is like visions from the past; therefore, unless something out of the ordinary happened, I would not remember. I was not bullied at school, and I must have been a prime subject for it unless it was tried and failed. I came from outside of town, and I daresay I was not dressed in good clothes. My mother used to say to us as long as your clothes are clean, you got nothing to worry about. And because the school did not allow children to go to school barefooted, it was alright to wear one sandal, and when one wore out, I wore the other one. I don't remember having any shoes except for the ones I borrowed for a show the school did in honour of the queen.

I did not like going to school, but I suppose I took it out on the teacher, especially one I remember well because I was in his class for three or four years; we only had one teacher to teach us all the subjects.

To start, I used to walk to school about a mile, and when I was wearing the right sandal, I used to find a stone or a tin and kick it all the way to school because I was right-footed.

I hated two things at school: to compensate for the starvation and the bombs, they used to give us a small glass of milk and a spoonful of cod liver oil because it tasted horrible. Luckily, sometimes I used to get a sweet from the boy that sat next to me. He used to bring a big bag of sweets every day because his parents owned a shop, and his teeth were green, but he used to give me the odd one when he felt like it, and I suppose I used to help myself when he went to the toilet.

Needless to say, air raids started when I happened to be walking to and from school. I stayed close to a wall until the planes passed and then I carried on, going nowhere to shelter. I think I started going to a big school but before long they put us in different houses. One was very different and very big; it was behind where McDonald's is today. It was also very spooky; some boys were afraid to go to the toilet on their own. Another house I went to was in front of the big school, and one of the boys was Michael, who later married my sister Rose. We had something in common because in the garden there was a big apricot tree; we used to take it in turns to go to the toilet and pick an apricot or two until the teacher realised that we were going too often to the toilet and that was the end of the apricots.

Not long after, we moved back to the big school. I remember I had the same teacher, a Mr Calleja, for three or four years; the headteacher was a Mr Grima. Mr Calleja was a good teacher and maybe a bit soft so as usual I tried to do my own thing, and when that happened, I was marched to the headteacher and punished. Sometimes it was a number of lines, and sometimes it was the cane and I pretended that it hurt. Mr Grima was the person to carry out the punishment.

When he used the cane, he used to pull faces. It happened very often. One particular time he was trying to get me to say something and kept hitting me with the cane for a long time; another day I remember he was sitting on his desk, and we were having some conversation, and I said something he did not like. He jumped out of his chair and ran towards me, I came out of my bench and ran back, and as I turned left behind the desks, he tried to kick me, but unfortunately for him he hit the bench. I must have had a few lashes of the cane for that.

I suppose I went to school to be educated, so I better say something about how I got on. I liked arithmetic, Maltese, and I think I liked geography because we learned a lot about the British Empire, and even today I like to know about other countries. I did not like many other subjects, so what I used to do when we were doing one of those was to start a new exercise book and put it under the desk and not give it to the teacher to check it. One day, we were doing one of these exercises, and the teacher was going round the class looking at us doing the work and said to me, 'Carm, you seem to have a new book for every subject,' so he checked for the other books and he found a lot missing, so I suppose that meant one more trip to headteacher.

I was very good with sums. When we had an exam, a new teacher used to come to do it and in later years used to write the sums in words. For example, a hotel had so many rooms with some guests paying five pounds a room, others paying different, some stayed longer than others and so on. When the teacher sat on his desk, I gave him my papers, and he always asked if I was sure that I was finished because he did not know me.

One day after school, I went to Ta Grezju field with my mother and must have got bitten by some insect, and my arm between my elbow and my hand was swollen like a balloon. So, next morning, my mother sent me to school and told me she'd come to take me to the doctor later that morning. I was called to go to the headteacher's office and my mother was there, and when the teacher saw my arm, he started having a go at my mother because she should have taken me to the doctor before, and I remember going to the doctor near the police station. As I was coming near the end of school, the headteacher sent for my mother and suggested to her because I was so good at sums, I should go and be an accountant, but all I wanted was to start earning some money. I was 14 years old.

Mensija Bar and Football Club –
small door around the corner

CHAPTER 4

THE STREET I LIVED IN

The street we lived in was the border between St. Julian and Birkirkara, so one side was St. Julian, and one side was Birkirkara, and the side I lived in was St. Julian. I was christened in St Julian's Church, and I love St Julian to this day.

The house I lived in belonged to my father's father. Sometime in his life, my grandfather leased a big field from the church and built his farm and two houses, he also leased some of the land to other people and kept a big field for himself. I lived in one of them; I will mention the connection later. The house had a garage, entrance hall, and a side room. Behind each room there was another room. In the garage was the water tap, in the room behind the entrance, there was a door that led to a small yard that had a room in it which was used as a kitchen. This consisted of a small room with a low ceiling, a small window and a workbench built with stones, and in the middle was a hole to use as an oven using wood. In the yard we had a grapevine and some flowerpots

There was a door that led to a bigger yard, and there were six rooms in that yard for animals. One of the rooms was dark and very spooky, we did not use it very much. I remember my mother used to keep meat in salt in a wooden box and other things she wanted to preserve because there were no fridges or freezers or electric lights so we used paraffin lamps. Of course, during the war we were in total darkness at night. Paraffin was used for lighting and cooking; a man used to come with a horse and cart with a tank on it, same with any supplies except bread. The bread man had a van and one day I pinched an item used to weigh, the bread and when my mother saw it, I had to put it back and so I did.

By now, I wonder if you're missing something in my house? Pause for a minute and think. I said we had a water tap in the garage and did not mention water again, so where was the bathroom? When I needed to go to the toilet, I grabbed a bit of paper and went to one of the rooms located for animals where my mother used to keep the manure, and that was our bathroom. It was also useful for the rabbits to make nests in it because we kept rabbits, chickens, a goat, and a couple of sheep. There was also a ghost in the house and the one next door. I will come to it later.

In Malta every child went for religion lessons, so I used to go to San Gwann Church only a few metres down the road, but as I got a bit older I started going to St. Julian. I went to this big house, it even had a basement. I liked it because sometimes they used to take us on outings, mostly to the seaside. One day, we went to Marsaxlokk; we were swimming on the rocks and I stepped next to a sharp rock and cut a big hole inside my right ankle. Another time, we went to Golden Bay, and with us we had this older boy dressed as a soldier and helping the teachers. Something happened involving the soldier, but I don't remember because as I said before these memories are like visions. And another time, we went to what at that time we called il qallet in St Julian's where the Hilton is today, and we swam near the rocks again, even though the sea was rough and we were still young.

By this time I had learned to swim, so I got in the sea and swam OK, but when I tried to get back on the rocks the waves kept pulling me under. When the soldier, as we used to call him, started shouting to swim back and as I got out to sea, he told me to look at the rocks and see where the waves were not rough hitting the rooks and to go in where you could see it wasn't rough and you would be alright, so I did and everything went well. That was the first time, and that could have avoided a disaster, but I learned a good lesson.

For some reason, the teachers decided to put me in charge of a class. I was down in the bottom basement and I had four to five children. I don't know what I taught them, religion or other things, because by now I had probably started with my mischief, but I will come to that later.

CHAPTER 5

FOOTBALL

As I said before, I kicked a stone or a thing all the way to school and back home, but the first game I remember could have been just after the war because the field we were playing in was next to the cart ruts and part of the area that used to be the ammunition dump. Because it was a small village, the team was a mix of different ages and I was probably the youngest and the smallest. The pitch wasn't very level and I think it was a bit on a slope and we put four stones as goalposts. The football we used at that time was made of leather with a bladder inside, and the hole you put the bladder through was laced with a leather string. The outside had to be greased to keep the water off because if it got wet, it would be very heavy. I remember the game. I was playing barefooted because I was saving my sandals to wear them for school, and my mother would not let me wear them. All I remember is that I was playing right-wing and I scored a goal; I don't know what the problem was because there was a big argument about the goal.

From that field, we moved to another better field which was more level. Unfortunately, it was next to a field that belonged to my uncle Toni who was a big man and a tyrant, so when we were playing he used to stay in the field and if the ball landed in the field he put a knife in it and threw it back to us, and that was the end of the game. Nobody was brave enough to say anything to him. From there, we moved across the road to another field that the farmer did not work anymore. By this time, I had left school and I had bought my first shoes so they were used for everything, including football. By this time, the team was organised with a coach and we had a small room to meet in. I was picked to play in every game we played, and I was good at scoring an odd goal. I remember one day I was playing and my foot came out of the side of the only pair of shoes I had, so I hopped home.

I used the skills I learned as a shoemaker, and after that I bought a pair of football boots. We became a decent team although some of the players could not kick the ball or play it but we were all keen and put in a good effort, and we used to play against some teams that played in the league.

San Gwann Football Team 1951

I was working in Gzira in a big block of flats and at lunchtime we used to play football. One day, this guy asked me if I wanted to play with Valletta under-eighteen team. Of course, I said yes, so we arranged to meet and he took me to the club where I met the coach and the staff and they agreed to give me a test in one of their games. They told me to go to the club the following Saturday or Sunday because I could be playing, so I did play and they told me that I would be playing for them, and I played in every game. Soon after, I took one of the players of the San Gwann team and he was accepted as well. After one of the players of San Gwann called Joe called a meeting about me playing with another team – not the other player; that's how Joe was – we were told to wait outside, and after a little while, the door opened and a big fight was going on because Joe wanted to throw me out of the club but not the other player, so the other players did not agree, and that's how the fight started. I am afraid he lived all his life doing and saying stupid things even when we were in England and worked with the same company, that's how I know because I used to have problems with him.

Back to football. The team threw Joe's argument out and I was back in the team and I could play for Valletta. We were playing one Sunday against Sliema, and the coach knew that me and my friend supported Sliema. He asked us if we wanted to play and we both said yes. The game started and I was having a very good game, I had a few shots at the goal and headers but I could not score. Towards the end of the game, a good pass came my way and the goalie and I dived for it, the goalie punched my neck and I headed the ball into the net.

As I was walking up the pitch, I remember coughing all the time the players were congratulating me. My friend did not play very well, and the coach told me that if it wasn't for me, he would have had a good hiding but he barred him from the club. Some of my friends used to come and watch me play and heard the other team coach, who was the best centre-forward Sliema ever had, saying how well I could read the game. The next morning someone told me that I was in the Maltese national paper, and in it was the good goal I scored. Because the game was between the teams that were from the two most popular towns, the press was there.

I finished the season, and one evening I was in Sliema and I met some of the boys from the San Gwann team and they suggested that I play for Sliema. I did not like the idea because Sliema was full of posh people and I would not be playing, but I was persuaded to go in. I remember we had to go upstairs, and as we got up, sitting on a chair there was this guy that came from San Gwann and lived a few doors from me. He did not spend any time in San Gwann, but because he was involved in football, I suppose he knew about me, so I signed for Sliema but I was not very happy.

Once at about 10 at night, the bell rang when we were all in bed so my mother opened the door. My mother came to my bedroom and told me that Joe and a couple of other guys wanted to see me, so I went to the door. I said hello to Joe and he said, 'This is my cousin; he is the coach of Balzan football team, and he asked me to show him where you live so he can have a word with you.'

He said, 'I know you signed with Sliema, but I would like you to play with us, and if you accept, I will do everything for your transfer.' Balzan was a small village a mile or two from my house. I accepted and asked him to let me know when I was needed. The season started and I played for San Gwann and Balzan, which was a friendly club. I played every game and was doing very well when I went for training which was only running but I loved it. We used to run towards Rabat and when the other players turned back, I used to keep going for a lot longer. I played every game, and each time before it started and the captains met in the middle of the pitch, I was called to go and speak to the referee who asked me my age because the other team made a complaint that I was older than 18. I think it was because I never used to shave before the game because of sweating and therefore I always had a beard.

When I finished the training, the buses were finished so I had to walk home. As I said before, it was about two miles away and in winter there was good and bad weather, but that was not the only problem. About half a mile from home, the road was full of roamers – that's thieves who used to jump on people as they walked by. So as I said before, I will return to the gun. Unknown to anyone, I used to take the gun with me when I went training, hidden in my raincoat and hoping nobody found it. As I came near this cross with an inscription, I could hear nothing and see nothing as it was fields on both sides of the road with high walls, so somebody could jump on you and you wouldn't have a chance to escape them. I made sure that I walked in the middle of the road with the gun just sticking out of the front of the raincoat so if somebody jumped, I would have time to shoot him before he got to me. I never saw anything so I never got in any trouble.

I return to San Gwann. I suppose you think a game is the same as any other game, so I mention one or two that stuck in my mind. For a small village, we were a very good team, and teams from big towns near us used to challenge us to teach us a lesson but unfortunately they did not always succeed. We used to play teams in the second division too; I remember it was Mosta and Birkirkara and we did well and they did not like it.

I must have played in every ground that existed at that time including the main stadium, and some of them were really rough with no grass. One game we played was at a ground in a big convent, and it must have rained very heavily because all along one side, half the ground was covered in 200mm of water. I was playing outside-right so for one half I was playing in water. I remember it must have been very hot because at half time, I was cooling down by washing my face in a barrel of water, there was no shower room.

That was against a team that belonged to one of the big towns, Paola, and it finished a draw but it was for a cup tie so we had to play them again. I remember playing them two more times and finishing with a draw, and the fourth time they beat us six–nil.

When a foreign team came to Malta to play a friendly in the main stadium, they used to put on a game before the big game started. So one day it happened to be Balzan versus Sliema, the coach did not have anybody to play outside-left so he asked me. A big game like that playing in front of a packed stadium and I had to play out of my position. I did not have a very good game, I only remember having one shot and that was with my left foot. In the second half, I was playing near where I used to sit when I went to watch football, so my friends were sitting there, and every time I touched the ball they started shouting 'traitor' at me, so some of the other spectators started shouting the same, so I am afraid it was not a very good day.

Going back to the San Gwann team, I mentioned two games that stayed in my mind. We were playing an important game against a team from Sliema in a ground that at that time we called St Andrews; today it is called Pembroke. We played there many times before, and it was the only ground that the pitch was red, of course it had goalposts and it was properly maintained.

It is still there today, but it is called something else. I think they have concerts and other shows there. I remember we were attacking towards where our spectators were, and I scored a goal, and for some reason the other players surrounded me complaining and my other players came to support me. In that confusion, I spotted my cousin Manwel He was easy to spot as he was six foot plus holding the ball. He was squeezing the ball so hard with temper that the ball was about 150mm instead of about 240mm. By the way, the goal was allowed, and the game carried on.

As it happens, I learned a lesson because of it a few days later. I was talking about the incident to some other boys, and one of the bigger boys must have thought I was boasting. I was talking about it because it was a strange thing to see, but out of the blue he told me, 'When you want to fart, you can only fart from your bottom.'

As I grew up to face the world, I remembered those words and what they meant; that when in trouble, you are on your own.

Another game that I remember well. A team from Sliema that we played before and thought they could beat us. They challenged us to play a game for a cup, so a cup was bought, and a game and ground was booked. The ground was in Gzira, walking distance from San Gwann in a school run by a priest. The pitch was properly run but the pitch was rough.

The day arrived and the preparation all done. It was a big occasion, and the whole village came to support us, not all the men knew about football, but everybody knew some of us if not all the players.

We all made our way to the ground, including builders, goat-keepers, cow-keepers and people that did know whether the football was square or round; they had never watched a football game but they come for the big game.

The team from Sliema was formed from a small area and did not have a lot of supporters, not like us. The game started and a few priests were watching the game. We were doing well, and nobody had scored by this time when one of our players from near the middle of the pitch for reasons unknown decided to kick the ball towards our own goal and he scored the best goal ever scored in that ground before or after, it was unbelievable. Nobody could believe what happened.

Our supporters started shouting and walking about with anger, and in that confusion, one man that had never come to watch us play before grabbed the cup, threw it on the floor and stamped on it. When one of their supporters started running towards the man and shouting, 'I am going to belt him to the ground,' unfortunately he went by the toughest man in our supporters. So as the man approached him, he punched him, and the man went down like a ton of bricks. I remember the priest ran in and appeared on the roof to watch, but we had a lot more supporters, so their supporters knew that if they started any fighting, they would be worse off. That stopped the game, and the priest barred us from playing in their ground again.

We all went home disappointed because we thought we had a good chance of winning the game. Tromy was the nickname of the guy that scored the disaster goal, and he could not explain what happened. I think the big game got to his mind and he got mixed up which way he was going, and so he shot at the wrong goal post.

We carried on playing and at first it was hard to find teams willing to play us because we got a bad name after the fight. After a while, the fight was forgotten and I continued to play for San Gwann and Balzan. If the game for Balzan was on a Saturday, I used to play for San Gwann on a Sunday and waited for Monday morning; I will mention it later.

The end of the last season arrived, and Balzan offered me to stay with them and play in the third division because by the start of next season I would be over 18, but my mind was on emigrating to Canada. After that, I continued to play only for San Gwann until I emigrated.

CHAPTER 6

THE WORKING YEARS IN MALTA

I was going to the fields when the war started and I was four years old. What work can you do in a field at that age? Not much, but winter was on its way and being there was bad enough. I am sure I could pick weeds from the floor when somebody else dug them out. At that time, we also had the air raids to contend with, we did not have anywhere to shelter when we were in Swieqi field, so in the beginning, we used to run to the bottom of the valley where there was a little cave. It was a big rush to get to the cave before the planes arrived. We used to hear the sirens from St. Julian's and run like hell. When I grew up a bit, I used to jump the dry walls, which were about six or seven foot high, but when you are running for your life you don't have time to think.

One day we did not hear the sirens but we heard the planes. By that time the German planes were nearly on top of us, so we took shelter the best we could under the nearest grapevine. As the planes were going over us, one left the formation and started to dive; it went down until it was practically landing when all of a sudden the machine gun started firing down towards the ground. As I followed to see what it was firing at, I could see a man running and unfortunately the man was shot down. The plane took off and started going up, but by this time it was very close to Ta Gorney fort, which started firing at it right away. It wasn't long before they shot it down and it was good to watch it burn. The pilot parachuted down, and a farmer who probably watched the whole saga soon captured him. Because I was on top of the hill, I had a very good view of it all.

After that episode, which my mother witnessed as well, she decided to hide under a big fig tree which we had in the top field because we had three fields, one above the other going up the hill.

When we were in the field Ta Grezju which was one of our three fields, during the war, we again had nowhere to shelter except a small stone room that I mentioned before and a big carob tree where we could hide. One day, the man in the next field asked as to shelter in his building, but when we arrived, the room had some of the roof missing and the rest was not much better. If a bomb had fallen near it, the lot would fall down, so that was the end of that and we made do with the stone room and the carob tree. Sometimes we used to go to a friend's house which was about quarter of a mile away across a lot of fields. It was hard for all of us, especially for my mother so we did not do that for long.

The war ended, and I became a proper farmer and expected to do what was necessary, which at that time was not a strange thing for children to do. In England, children aged seven and younger used to go down the mines and work in the cotton mills, which was a terrible job to do; children ended up being crippled, so the work I was doing was not too bad and working morning or afternoon, very rarely we worked all day.

So, with six fields to cultivate, everything had to be done by hand except ploughing. My mum, John and me had a lot to contend with, but after school and Saturday we managed to produce a good crop which helped to maintain the family with food money and food for the animals.

Some of the work was very hard and back-breaking and they were long days, especially when we were hoeing a big field of potatoes and what we called heaping, which means when the potatoes are forming they had to be covered; otherwise they'd go green and would be no good.

Another job that was harder was cutting wheat. When it was harvest time, I had to bend right down and cut the wheat with a sickle and keep looking to see how

San Gwann Football Team 1952

far I had to go. So we had to make sure that the sickle was very sharp. Another crop we had to cut was called silla, it was harder than the wheat. If you ever go to Malta at the beginning of summer, you might notice a crop with red flowers in the fields that would be silla. The farmers feed it to the animals; it had thicker and harder stems; my mother used to grow it to feed the rabbits, goat and the sheep.

A farmer used to take the wheat and turn it into wheat and straw; I will explain later. Mum used to pay somebody to take the silla to our house on a horse and cart.

Every time we went to the fields, we had to take all the weeds and some crops and carry them all the way home. From Swieqi, we used to go up by Mensija

Church and when I say go up, it was all uphill; I was sweating and it was very hard on the legs after some hours of hard work.

Talking about Mensija Church, it is a nice church with an interesting story. The story goes that a farmer found a picture of the Virgin Mary in a cave, and the church authorities took it to Birkirkara church because at that time Mensija was the limits of that parish.

According to rumours, the picture returned to the cave three times so the local people decided to build the church. In olden times, people used to build a church for all sorts of reasons, one the reasons was in the days of the pirates people used to hide wherever they were and made a wish to a saint or the Virgin Mary to build a church.

Castello Lanzon

Mensija Church

THE KNIGHTS' HALL

Castello Lanzon was built in the fifteenth century, and in my time was occupied by a farming family, and it was well known for having a ghost. It was said that the family had a young baby which they used to put to sleep in a hammock, and sometimes the parents used to see a man swinging the hammock.

Today it is the headquarters of the Knights of St. Lazarus of Jerusalem, I found information about the Castello on the internet, but unfortunately, I did not find anything about the church in English. It's a good story in Maltese.

As I am writing about my working life, I will continue. Besides helping my mother in the fields, I also helped my uncles and my cousin Emanuel. Besides being farmers, they also did haulage using a horse and cart because after the war there were a lot of bombed buildings to be cleared. I only remember going with Uncle Wenzu – he was married to Aunt Janna – only once, and that was in Sliema. I remember exactly where the house was we were clearing; it was as we were driving on Tower Road, going towards the ferries, we passed the Preluna Hotel on the right, you turn first left, and the house was a few metres on the right. I think I remember we were loading and tipping the rubble across the road and into the sea; it was hard, all we were doing was loading and unloading. I used to go with my Uncle Emanuel, and I remember he used to go and unload in the sea in a place called il fortina Today this place is known as Tigne. Another place we used to unload is alieb. It was where the Hilton Hotel is today. Sometimes after work, he used to put the horse in the sea and we also had a swim. Manwel used to teach me to swim, and that is where I learned to swim on the rocks.

I used to spend a lot of time with Emanuel as he had no children. He had a lot of fields in Swieqi where we had the fields, New Swieqi and Wied Għomor, it meant life valley, and he had a lot of carob trees. When it was harvest time, my uncle, his wife, and one or two others used to do it, and because I was the youngest, my job was to go up the branches and harvest the carob. It was not very easy and sometimes it was dangerous, and it used to take about a week to do the lot.

Another time we were at Wied Għomor, valley of long life, to cultivate one of the fields. The horse just fell to the floor and died. My uncle did not know what to do. You can imagine how he felt because he was a lovely horse and my uncle was very keen on horses, especially on that horse because he used to take it to shows where it won three times. The first prize was a palio, a sort of long downwards flag, and he always gave it to St Julian's Church, and they used to carry them in the procession on feast day; he also used to carry the statue of St. Julian.

Before the day of the show, my uncle used to wash the horse and make fresh bedding for him. Me and my aunt used to plait the horse's hair; my aunt used to do the tail, and after a lot of begging, I used to stand on a box and do the hair on its neck and my uncle used to do the hair on the horse's face.

Next morning, we got up very early and started preparing the horse for the show. I undid some of the plaits and then I was not allowed to go near the horse because they wanted to finish the horse themselves. When they finished, the horse looked beautiful, they put the horse and cart together and off we went to the show. I do not remember where they used to hold the shows because I was still very young when all this was happening.

After the horse died, my uncle needed to buy another horse. What used to happen when you needed to buy a horse or a mule or a donkey was that they used to import these wild animals from North Africa, put them in a farm as they arrived and open the sale. The animals used to be in rooms full of horseflies and in a right state, very skinny, dirty, and full of flies. So when you looked at one of these animals, you had to use your imagination. My uncle had a good eye for horses and again he picked an all-black one to replace the horse that died, he got the horse home, gave it a good wash and a good feed.

My uncle's horse that I used to get ready for the show

Next morning, he put the harness and cart on the horse, which the horse did not like and started to jump and tried to run away, but my uncle held on, and the horse settled down and was very good after it filled out, and it became a beautiful animal. I said how hard it was to harvest the wheat and someone used to come to take it away to turn it into wheat and straw. There was no machinery at that time, so what used to happen was the farmers used to find a suitable bit of ground, it had to about 12 metres round in the open, so to get a bit of wind to sift the wheat, wet the ground up and roll it and leave it to get hard.

I remember one year, my uncle made one of these which was called qijja, so when the harvest was done, we put some of the wheat we had cut on it and made the horse go round and round on it until all of it was thrashed, and separated the wheat from the straw. When it was done, we threw it in the air with a special tool which looked like a fork, sometimes you see the odd one in a country restaurant, we threw the thrashed straw high according to how high the wind was to keep the straw in a reasonable heap. When all the straw was cleared, the wheat was sifted and put in sacks and the straw tied in bales. A couple of things I experienced that year; it was the first and last time I got on a horse when the horse was going round and round. My uncle put me on the horse, and of course I enjoyed that.

One day we were having a sleep at midday near the qijja sheltering from the sun when something woke me up wiggling in my pants, so I got up screaming and jumping and woke my uncle and aunt up. Of course, they started laughing at my jumping, and a mouse fell out of my shorts.

One day we were in New Swieqi harvesting the grapes, and my uncle said to me, 'Next year, I buy you a small donkey and you can go and sell the grapes in Sliema.'

So I said, 'I will try to make the harness myself.' I looked in his buildings for anything I could use and there was some stuff left in our house from my father's horse, so with the skills I learned from working in the shoemaker shop and looking at other donkeys and carts, I made one. I don't know how long it took me because I was still going to school but I finished and looked forward to getting a donkey – wishful thinking – I must have done a good job at that age because the next thing I heard was that my uncle sold it to a friend.

That's how my life was – lots of disappointments. Besides that, my uncle was terrible to my family, never gave us any help carrying produce from Swieqi although he had a horse, and sometimes even when he was there, he never helped us to carry it home. He used to give the neighbours bags of fruit, but even passing our door, he never gave us nothing.

One day, I was in the field at the back of his house where he had lots of grapevines and other fruits, and I cut a small bunch of grapes. He had a go at me and told me that I would come out of my inheritance. He kept his word because he left me nothing. I did not spend a lot of time around my Uncle Jamri because you already heard what kind of a man he was with the football.

The things I remember worth mentioning. One day I was in Gamri's house, he was cutting the grapes to send to the market and as he was cutting, he was taking the bad grapes and putting them in a tin. I picked some from the tin and he told me to put it back as it was for the chicken, but he never gave me another bit to eat, how nice.

Another day I was there, another farmer brought one of his pigs to be mated with one of his pigs. One of the pigs tried to run away, and I remember the pig running round the field with Gamri trying to stop it; by the time the pig was finished, the field was full of ruts. It must have been summer because the field was empty.

Another day I went with my uncle on his horse, which he bought not a long time before and he was still afraid of cars, to deliver a bag of potatoes to a bank manager in Valley Road – the main road that went from Valletta to the north and west of Malta in Birkirkara. As it happened, the bank was opposite a main bus stop. My uncle took the bag of potatoes into the bank and left me holding the horse. Three buses started to move together and made a lot of noise, and when the horse heard that, it bolted, and as I held on to its reins, it kept lifting me and throwing me forward. All the people at the bus stop started shouting for me to let it go. After it took me about 30 metres, I let it go, so it ran amongst the traffic for about a quarter of a mile and turned left. We ran to where it went and found it in a quiet road. I was friends with my cousin Emanuel, he was huge like his father and he used to work some fields. After the war, he used his father's horse to do some haulage and I used to go with him. He would not let me help because I got in the way, and I remember clearing rubble from near a shelter they dug in Birkirkara. When we arrived, we had to wait because there were a few carts waiting to load. I remember he looked for the two big stones and nearly filled the box on the cart with other men telling him not to lift the stones because they were too heavy.

The box was made as big as possible to fit on the cart and about 400mm high; the back of the box could be lifted to make it easier to load.

Apart from rubble, he also carried freshly made floor tiles from Gzira. One day, we had a delivery to Sliema, which meant going up Savoy Hill, which was very steep, so he decided to go by Sliema ferries and up Prince of Wales hill, and although it wasn't as bad as Savoy Hill, it was longer. He thought the horse would not make it, so he found a stone and told me to carry the stone, and if the horse stopped, I should put the stone behind the wheel to stop the cart going down the hill. Luckily the horse did not stop, and I am here to write about it, because if it had happened, I would have been under the cart and the horse.

Not long after that, he bought an old Ford lorry and all I remember was when we finished work, he used to park it top of Mensija Road where his sister lived, and the road was full of holes, so every time we went down a hole, his head hit the roof of the cabin because he was such a big man.

Me at sixteen at the Carnival

Outing to Gozo

CHAPTER 7

MY FATHER'S FAMILY

My father's family were also farmers, most of their land was in a place called Swieqi and what they called New Swieqi. Of course, today it is a big town. Most of the fields were worked by my uncles because my grandfather was very old by then. And most of Swieqi was worked by interconnected families except for one area in the south where today there are a lot of villas, which was owned by a brother of my aunt. Where all my parents and the rest of the family had the fields, we used to share a big well that was at the lower field. So, unfortunately, we used to carry every drop of water up to our field from practically the bottom of the valley to the top of the hill where our field was. By the well, there was a room below and a room above it, and we had a share of the bottom room where we could put the tools and other things such as crops. I should mention the same fields later. As a second job, my father was a haulier partner with his brother using one horse. Besides working together, he used to work in their fields. One of the jobs they used to get was to load sand from a beach near Pebble Beach, and it was illegal to pick the sand from the beach because it was a small beach. And I know this because in later years my cousin Emanuel was a haulier, and he used to go and pick sand from the same beach, and I used to go with him as a boy to be his lookout when it was loaded and taken to a building site. Back to my father; as he loaded the sand and was going back to one of the towns to download it, he used to pass by my mother's home, and that is how he met my mother. The way people met in those days was through an intermediate person who was called Hattab and he was an estate agent; if you wanted to buy or sell anything, you would talk to Hattab. As it happens, one was involved when I was selling the flat I had in Malta in 2018.

CHAPTER 8

THE TRAGEDY

On that terrible afternoon of 15 August 1938, my uncle Joseph sold a hunting dog to a Gozo man who settled in San Gwann. A few years earlier, he was known as Salvu the bitch, a nasty man, the saying was that he was very cruel to the dog so it kept running home to my uncle's house. My uncle and the sister were fed up with the dog, which kept running back every time it escaped, so my uncle offered to buy the dog back but Salvu did not want to sell it. One afternoon on the fifteenth of August, Salvu went to Mensija Bar and told my uncle the dog had run away again and to go and bring the dog back. My uncle told him to go and ask his sister to give it to him. An argument started and Salvu shot my uncle, my father tried to take the shotgun from Salvu, and he shot one of my father's knees.

After the shooting, Salvu went to Gzira police station and reported the incident. He went to court, and his lawyer put the case that the shot did not kill my father but the tetanus did, he was found guilty, but he did not hang because of the tetanus argument but was sentenced to life in jail.

When I was about 16 years old, I was working in Sliema with a man called Joe the billy goat, I will mention him later He told me that Salvu was out of prison and living in St Julian, but he was dying of syphilis, and that was the last I heard of Salvu.

My Father and Uncle

The scene of the shooting affray. The boards mark the spot where Joseph Micallef stood. The shadow in the right bottom corner marks the approximate spot from where Mellak is alleged to have fired the shot. (Inset). Paul Debono, who witnessed the whole incident and who is stated to have been threatened by Mellak.

CHAPTER 9

MY GHOST STORIES

IT started when I was young when I was in bed, I could see near the water tap in a sort of a niche, and I used to see a man sometimes dressed as a scarecrow standing there. In the morning, I used to tell my mother, but she told me I was imagining things.

As you remember, in my mother's story, I mentioned what happened to me the night they were cutting the potatoes. I woke up in the middle of the night, and next to the bed there was a man sitting near to my face, staring at me. He was wearing a white shirt with lines going down. I covered my head and tried to go to sleep, and as soon I heard my mother talking, I jumped out of bed to tell her what I had seen. All of them looked at each other and did not say anything at first because the couple that were helping my mother used to live in our house before us, and they had trouble with the ghost themselves. Eventually, one told me that I was dreaming but I don't think I was. After that day, I started to notice strange things.

I mentioned the strange animal room, we used to call it the dark room, and when someone gave us a pair of pigeons, I put them in that room. I was afraid to go and feed them because it was scary, and I never liked going in that room even when I got older, and one day the pigeons disappeared. Out of nowhere, this big black cat used to appear and it had no boundaries in the house or in the small yard with the chickens, and the chickens were not scared of it. One day, it was in the house and my mother chased it out into the yard, and it jumped straight onto the roof, which was about seven feet high. I can remember my mother arguing with Marie very often that my mum left something on a shelf or in a cupboard and it was not there anymore, and after a day or two it was there again.

Just before we moved to the new house, one night me and John were in Mensija Bar with some friends, and John decided to go home. He came back in a hurry and told me to go home. I said I would come in a minute, but John kept on, and one of the friends told me I better go because it sounded urgent.

As we were on the way, I asked John what the problem was, and he told me my mum was scared and crying because she'd seen a man in the room that she and Marie slept in. So there I was, a fourteen-year-old boy, to sort this man out, although we thought it was the ghost, still there was nobody else to call for help, so I had to put on a brave face and go to see my mother. She told me she'd seen a man in the room and Marie said that my mum started screaming and scared the life out of her; my mum told me that the man disappeared into the wardrobe or under the beds.

Although I realised it was the ghost, I went and found the gun which was always loaded and like a brave man I started looking for the man under the beds, in the wardrobe, and all over the house, so I told my mother that there was no man any were. The gun would do nothing to the ghost, but I felt better holding it.

At the time, builders were working on our new house across the road and my mother told the builder, who was a distant relation of my father, to finish as soon as possible so we could move in because of what happened. I think the builder put more men on the job, and the house was finished and it was time to move in. So because we had some animals, my mother decided to leave me and John to stay and guard the animals. My mum and Marie moved in as soon as it was possible and me and John stayed the night. As it was summer, we slept in the small yard like we used to do on other nights but, of course, with the gun under my pillow.

In the middle of the night, with his elbow in my ribs, John woke me up, whispering in my ear, 'Somebody is in with the chickens.' So I listened and the chickens started flapping their wings as if somebody was disturbing them. Me and John looked at each other and ran in, taking a ladder with us as we went in and locked the back door. By this time, John, who was only 12 years old, looked very scared, so for his sake, I kept a brave face.

On top of the back door there was a small window, so I decided to put the ladder up so we could look out of the window and take it in turns to get on top of the ladder and see what was happening in the back yard. It was John's turn, and as soon as he got up the ladder, he told me that he could see a light going up the back wall, so I went up the ladder and saw nothing. By this time, John was getting very confused, but when I was trying to comfort him, we heard something that sounded as if somebody had kicked the tin my mother used to feed the chicken against the wall. I ran up the ladder, but again I did not see anything.

This went on for a while, and as I was up the ladder because John did not want to go up anymore, he decided to go in my mum's bedroom. I could hear him trying to open the door and the door would not open, and when he could not open the door, I said to him that the door was not locked because there was nothing in the room, so he challenged me to open it. So I just turned the handle and the door opened spontaneously. John spewed his guts out, so I realised that John had had enough, and I said to him, 'We better go to sleep and don't worry about the chickens.'

So, we went to sleep on my bed, terrified, of course. Next morning when we told my mother, she told us that we should have gone to the new house anyway, so we took the rest of the furniture and moved into the new house.

Some days after, we went to Swieqi, very early in the morning when it was still dark and the road was mostly in the fields, sometimes it used to be very scary and we used to hear funny noises, and sometimes we used to see different images that we could not explain, so we started to go a different way.

CHAPTER 10

THE BORG FAMILY

One day I was with Nick at his shop and a farmer came to buy some food for his animals, but Nick told him he could not deliver that day as he had nobody to drive the horse. So the farmer looked at me and said, 'I can take the loaded horse,' and pointing at me he said, 'He can bring the horse back.' Nick was hesitant because it was a racing horse, but he asked me and I accepted. So they loaded the horse and we went to his house, which was near where Mater Dei Hospital is today. So I got on the cart and started going back. I came to an old, abandoned house, which was partly fallen down, and as we approached the house, which was on the left, the horse moved to the right as near to the wall as possible and hesitated to go past the house, so I got scared. As soon as we passed the house, the horse bolted and ran towards his house as fast as it could, with me holding to the cart the best that I could. We arrived, and when Nick saw the horse all sweating, he asked me why it was sweating and I told him what had happened.

He told me that there were a lot of stories about a ghost in that house and somebody was murdered there, and a lot of people talked about it.

The Borg family: the father's name was Nik, short for Nicolas, and the mother's name was Carmina. They were a big family; there were two older girls, then there was Spiro and Zareen, short for Nazarene, teenagers, and there were two girls my age and younger, and then there were two younger boys. All the boys were very nice. I think the mother was very good and the girls followed her. Sometimes the young girls used to call John and me black just because we were a bit darker than them. They had the only toy I had ever seen at that age, it was a board game they bought; it was a brown board with an edge and round on top. Inside it had lots of pins and a small iron ball that you shot with a spring up the board; it was the only game I played that I did not make myself.

It was traditional to celebrate Easter with a swing, so Spiro and Zareen used to invite the boys from the village and make a swing. From the yard to the field, they had a very high door which was very handy for the swing. They used to throw a rope over the top, put a long plank on it and all sit on it and go as high as possible, and because the door was very tall, it was easy for them to go high. The boy at the front and at the back sat looking in opposite directions, so they made the swing go higher. One day as they were in full swing, the rope broke and luckily for them, they landed in a big fig tree, which was about 10 metres away, it softened the fall and nobody was hurt, but after that, Nik stopped the swing for good.

Nik had a business selling food for animals from the shop and delivered to farmers. Nik was always in the shop, and after I stopped going to Rose's house, I used to spend a lot of time with him or went with Spiro delivering to the farmers on a horse.

Just after the war, he started importing carob and other animal food from Spain. The carob was machined into small bits, and unlike Maltese carob, it was very thick and full of sugar, and Nik never stopped me from having a few to eat. Another food he used to get had nuts out of the shell in it, and I used to look for them as well. That used to be my sweets.

As the business increased and Spiro was old enough, they bought a Bedford lorry and Austin van and of course the horse, which they used to race in special races, like the feast of Santa Maria that the feast that my father went to on his last day, and Tony was the jockey.

Spiro used to take me with him everywhere, loading from the docks and delivering. In the summer when the farmers picked their crops, Nik and Spiro used to take me with them to go to the country to buy the animal food, load it on the lorry and move on. Some farmers did not have anything to sell, so sometimes we had to do a lot of driving which I enjoyed very much. To me, it was like an outing; we used to go to different parts of the country, north and west.

One day, I felt like asking Nik for one of the Maltese cigar dog-ends he used to smoke because all I smoked was dried potato leaves. So I got a bit of courage, and I asked Nik if I could have one of his dog-ends because sometimes he used to smoke some of the cigar and save the rest. He kept insisting on giving me a whole one, but I was too embarrassed so we settled for a dog-end. He lit it up for me and I started to smoke, but before long I started to realise why he wanted to give me a whole cigar. My stomach started to feel funny, then I started feeling sick, so I started running to a field Nik had behind the shop, and before long, everything started pouring out of everywhere. After a while, I went back to Nik, and with a smile on his face, he told me that I should have taken his advice.

Spiro used to go hunting to the other side of Malta, such as to Intahlep, the limits of Bahrija, and Salib Tal Lolja, which means the high cross limits of Rabat. We used to go in the Austin van, and sometimes he used to leave me in the van while he went shooting. As soon as he went and disappeared in the fields, I used to start the van using a bit of wire connecting a couple of screws together under the dashboard and started the engine and kept driving backwards and forwards until I got fed up.

One day Spiro had to deliver a load of manure to Mellieha to some farmer, and although it was a five-ton lorry, Spiro loaded as much manure in sacks as high as he could. Everything was going all right until we started going up the Mellieha hill, he tried to go up in second and it could not cope. By this time, I started wondering if we were going to make it. Spiro put it in first gear and kept going uphill at walking pace with the engine singing like a bird and in agony. After what to me felt like a lifetime, we got to the top of the hill without any problems.

As if that was not enough, when we arrived near the fields the manure was going in, we had to go up what looked a steeper hill again because Spiro was worried, told me to stay away, put the truck in first gear and went up the hill.

As the boys got older, they used to get up to some shady things, so they used to go to Gzira and a bar in Salina Bay limits of Naxxar at night, and they used to take me with them as an alibi so their parents wouldn't ask any questions, and I used to wait in the lorry.

One day, the boys and some of their friends from the village were going to Mellieha for the feast of Santa Maria, so they filled the lorry up with petrol from tins because I don't think there were any petrol stations at that time. When the boys were standing by the lorry ready to go, one decided to light a cigarette, threw the match on the floor and the petrol on top of the tank and on the flour around the tank caught fire. You could imagine the panic! All of a sudden, my cousin Emanuel grabbed a hessian sack and smothered the petrol tank and stopped the flame and the petrol on the floor burned out. What a scare; apparently they went to the feast, got drunk and did a lot of damage to the feast decorations, so we heard after; this is one of the things that stuck in my mind. As time passed by, Spiro got engaged to Teresa, so he started to behave himself, but I kept going with him during the day. One day we went to the docks and took his future brother-in-law, French, short for Frangisco. Zareen and Nik met us on the dockside in Marsa. They left us in the lorry, and they left the keys in the lorry, so when they left, me and French took it in turns to drive the truck forwards and backwards. We had to be very careful because there was no barrier in front of us straight into the sea. I was driving when we saw them across the sea coming back. I panicked and put my foot on the accelerator instead of the brakes; quick-thinking French grabbed the handbrake and pulled as high as he could. The lorry stopped, and our lives and the lorry were saved for the second time. After that, Spiro and Teresa got married and went to England, and I went to find other things to amuse myself.

CHAPTER 11

MY DOG

After the war I decided to get a dog. I do not know how my mother let me have it because we barely had food for us, but I think she thought I would settle down because by now I had started to get out of control. My dog's name was Brimbo, similar to a spider because when he was young, all you could see was four legs sticking out. It was a mongrel, a Labrador and something else; it grew to 300 or 400mm.

Because of the chicken, unfortunately, I used to keep it on the roof of the kitchen because it was lower than the other roofs. While I was writing, this book I was suddenly asked how I used to take the dog up the ladder at that age. It was a lovely dog and very good to handle. When I took it to the fields, he used to have a nibble of everything, some grass, grapes if in season, and figs, and it never used to do any damage.

One day I decided to do a harness and a cart for it, and after a while I made them, and they fitted very well.

I started putting them on him, and he didn't like being confined, but after a while he settled down, and he used to stay still while I was getting it ready. When I went to Ta Grezju field, sometimes I used to take the dog pulling the cart as we went along. One afternoon, we were in the shade under a big carob tree we had in one corner of the field, and about one hundred metres away the other side of the field we had a fig tree. All of a sudden, a guy came and started pinching some figs, so I started shouting. The dog started barking, and suddenly it took off after the robber with the cart flying up and down; by the time the dog got halfway up the field, the cart was in a hundred pieces and by the time it got to the fig tree, the robber was over the dry wall, and the dog was then off the cart.

Other boys had dogs as well, and we decided to start racing them because we all thought our dog was the best of all the others. So we found the bit of Naxxar Road that was straight and decided the distance, and one boy held one dog and the owners stayed at the finish line calling their dogs. I shouted Brimbo and the dogs were let loose and ran towards us. Brimbo always managed to come first or second, but the other boys always complained about my dog winning so they insisted that we race them again. One night we must have raced the dogs a few times because after I got home, the dog died, and I never had another dog.

CHAPTER 12

MY TOYS

Of course, I had never seen any toys, never mind having some, so the thing was to make my own, and somehow I was good at it, like I made the dog's cart. The first toy I remember making was from a fish tin, it was about 250mm by 150mm with one end rounded and about 50mm deep, and at the other end, the corners were rounded. I don't think they are sold today. I cut four wheels from two cotton reels, but I do not remember how I connected the wheels to the tin. All I used to do was go where I could find some dust and move it from one spot to another. Sometimes, I used to go in the room where we kept animal food, filled the tin with the food and cart it around the room; I suppose I used to imitate my uncles doing haulage.

My speciality was carts and scooters. I think I used to make sure that I lined the wheels up properly, which the other boys did not do.

Because I used to go with my uncles to clear bombed houses, it was easy to find wood, sometimes bits of oak. I don't remember where I used to get the wheels from for the carts and scooters. I used to use ball bearings. I barely remember trying to explain to somebody what I was looking for, maybe it was a garage, but I don't remember there being any garages at that time because there was only about three cars in the whole village, only horses and carts.

I took pride in making them while my mother complained about me making them because they were dangerous. I suppose you, like me, are wondering where I used to get the material for them because there was no B&Q or even a hardware shop then. We only used nails at that time, I do not know if screws existed then. Of course, I used to recycle nails, and if I found a piece of wood with nails in it, I took it home, took the nails out and straightened them to reuse them.

I have no idea where I got the forks for the scooters from, maybe my cousin Manwel helped me with them. The scooter I made to my size, and the cart was smaller than the one I used to pinch the shells with, it was about 500mm wide and about 600mm long. Where I sat was a strong piece of wood in the middle going from the back to the front, and sticking out of the seat about 300mm out in front, connected to it, I had a bit of wood about 250mm long that was to steer with. Underneath, I had one wheel. Sometimes, we used a bit of string connected to the two ends of the wood and sometimes I used to sit on the cart and steer it with my feet according to what I was trying to do or race. Before I say what I used to do with the cart and scooter, I would like you to remember that apart from horses there was hardly any traffic on the roads, so unlike my mother, I did not think it was too dangerous. That is, apart from the man who gave the black trousers to my mother for my performance for the show for Empire Day. I heard after that he was a big building contractor and that he built a big theatre in Gzira and it was beautiful. He had a big Austin car, it must have been the biggest they made at that time, it was painted black and was the only car in San Gwann. The only thing was, he could not drive it, he used to drive from one side of the road to the other. I was so terrified of him that one day I was on my scooter going down in front of San Gwann Church and I saw him coming from Birkirkara. I got so excited that I fell off the scooter; anyway, he used to go only for a short drive and a lot of the time I used to see him coming back with his brother, towing the car with his horse.

If I went for a ride on the cart, I sat on my side so I could push the cart with my leg and steer the cart with the string. To practise for the races, I used to get on top of a hill, get on the scooter or the cart and let go, hoping nothing got in the way, especially if I turned round the corner and saw how far it got on its own.

Now when I did this on the cart, it was more dangerous because I sat on the cart and steered it with my feet, so no sandals. I started in front of San Gwann Church and let it go, turned right at the bottom of the hill where the road was flat and if I made it, thank God I always made it, and I stopped near the house where the English flag was first raised in Malta. Of course, the higher up the hill you start, the more dangerous and the longer you go.

CHAPTER 13

THE RACES

One of the races was when we pushed the carts ourselves, and it used to happen in Naxxar Road, starting from where the roundabout is today to where the road meets the main road coming from the right. I would like you to know that was beastly because a lot of horses and carts loaded with stones from Tal Ballal to go to Sliema used the road, and probably it was not tarmacked, so full of holes which we had to navigate. It was not my favourite race. One of the races I used to like because it tested my capability of making the carts and scooters and my ability of handling them was when we used to use San Gwann hill and, as I said before, two at a time, we let the carts go and saw who got to where, which cart stopped first, and who went the farthest. Of course, if I won, like the dog, they said that I cheated, but when I looked at the wheels, they were not lined up.

One of the reasons for that was that we used wooden shafts because the ball bearing wheel hole was about 50mm, and we had to hammer the wood into the hole of the wheel, and if you were not careful, you hammered one side more than the other and the wheel would not be straight, and it slowed the cart or scooter down.

When you sit on the cart, steering with your feet, no brake, you have nothing to stop the cart, you have to wait for it to stop or have an accident. With the scooter, at least you can put your foot down to stop it. We were not that clever at that age to fit brakes, so it was a bit of dare-devilling because when we turned right at the bottom of the hill, if somebody was coming from the left, we could not do anything about it except get run over.

The hill at San Gwann got a bit boring so we started looking further and further for better and steeper hills until eventually we got to Madliena Hill, which was about five miles away from San Gwann overlooking Penbrook and Baħar iċ-Ċagħaq. It was a very steep hill leading to the main road from St Julian's and Sliema to Pebbles Beach and St. Paul's Bay.

Even for that time being a very narrow road, it could be busy because all that area was occupied by the British Army which had jeeps and lorries. But that did not worry us, so we decided where to start from the hill, got on the carts, put our feet on the steering and went down, hoping that nothing got in our way. Of course, we used to be lucky, and thank God I am here to tell you all about it. Whenever somebody told my mother that they saw me doing something dangerous, my mother went into a breaking mood and broke my cart and scooter. Luckily, she did not throw away the things that were hard to get, so I would make them again only better than before and ready to start again. I think I left them in one of the rooms when I left for England for John to throw away when he decided to have a clear out.

CHAPTER 14

MY BIRDS

When my father died, he left us a relic. It was a big cage put against the ceiling in the room that led to the yard. It was about 600mm by 1 metre by 700mm high. Of course, because it was high and heavy, we left it until we could climb up the ladder and get it down because my mother would not touch it. So I think it was just after the war when we got it down, and we found bird skeletons on the floor of the cage and even smaller skeletons in the nest. I think he used to breed canaries. I do not know what happened to the cage but we did not have it any longer.

So, I got the urge to have some birds, only I could not afford canaries so I settled for sparrows. I managed to get a nest of five baby sparrows. I put them in one of mum's wicker baskets and when they grew, I put them in a cage. Luckily, they all survived, and I used to let them out of the cage indoors and they used to go back in the cage when it was time for food.

So it was time to take my chance and try them in the yard. I took the cage in the yard, opened the cage and waited to see what was going to happen. The first one got out and flew up to the grapevine, and one after the other they got out and rested on the grapevine and looked around. It was not long before the first flew onto the roof and the rest followed, with me crying my eyes out; by this time probably I was about 10 or 11 years old. So, I decided to try to catch some sparrows. I managed to get a net from a man who lived in front of San Gwann Church who used to make them. The net was about a metre and half by about 800mm, the middle was loose, so there was room for the birds if any were caught.

To trap the birds, we used to make a hole under a tree because it was easier to make it somewhere I could hide, and fill the hole with water. I don't remember how I used to seal it. I had set the net and wait for the birds to come for a drink and hopefully to catch them, and sometimes I did. I had one hole near the big fig tree in Swieqi field and one under the big carob tree we had in Ta Grezju field.

As luck had it, in the corner of the room that I did not like going in against the roof, there was what is called an aviary that my father must have done. It had a hole going into a small cage outside so the birds could go in it, so I put the birds that I caught in it. I remember

I was very ill when I was 10 or 11 years with a high temperature, so I asked my mother to feed my birds, but she would not. So with her screaming, I put some clothes on and went to feed them myself, that's how I remember my age because of my illness. I think I had yellow fever. When I started work, I got rid of the sparrows and started to get some singing birds and kept them till I left for England.

CHAPTER 15

VISITING MY MOTHER'S BROTHERS AND SISTER

I barely remember my grandad because he was very old and not very well and in bed, and I think I only saw him a few times before he died; he was a small man and a very nice person. As soon as John could manage the walk to my uncles, who lived in Pebbles Beach, which was about six miles away from home, some Sundays we used to go and visit them.

When I knew that we were going, and although it was that far, I really looked forward to it because they looked after us very well and it was so different from what we were used to, especially in summer. It was near the sea and my uncles made use of it. They used to have ready for us urchins, limpets, and other fish that they had caught the day before. They had all sorts of fruit growing in their fields, melons, watermelons and, unlike my father's brothers, they never stopped telling us to have whatever we wanted. They really made us welcome, it was such a different atmosphere. Sometimes I used to go with Uncle Mikael to the sea, which was only a few metres away from where they used to live, and get some urchins and limpets, and he'd buy me an ice cream if they were around, which was the only time I would have one.

We did not go in winter, so we only went when the weather got better, but we all looked forward to the time to come.

The farmhouse where they lived was on the main road although there was very little traffic passing by, especially at weekends.

The house consisted of six rooms for animals, a big yard, a small yard, and one big room upstairs, and that was for living and sleeping. They had a garage, a small yard behind it, and two of the animals' rooms; one where they kept their mule and the other where they kept two very rare Maltese cows. In 2010, the authorities found that there were only three of these cows left in the whole of Malta, which they found by chance, no bull, so they used a bull from Sicily which resembles the Maltese cows to start the race going again. All the roofs in the farmhouse were flat like all the roofs in Malta.

As you go through the front door in most farmhouses in Malta, you go into a yard, but this was a bit different. You went into the front door, and in front of you there was a gap and a gate that led to the big yard, and immediately to your left, there were the stairs going to the top room. As you reached the door on the left, there was a narrow path leading to all the flat roofs. As you can imagine, it was a bit dangerous because it was only about 400mm wide and about six metres long to the first roof.

When we went at the end of summer, all the roofs used to be carpeted by dried figs and dried tomatoes, they used to have wooden boxes full of them and, of course, we used to get a fair share of them as well, all ready for the winter.

Besides the mule and cows, which they used to plough the fields, and the mule to use with the cart to move the crops, in summer in the field in front of the farmhouse, they used to have the wheat thrashing ring, and they used the mule and the cows to do the thrashing. It is very old fashioned to use the cows to cultivate the fields; I have never seen cows being used for that before or after in Malta. Because there was nowhere to shelter from the sun in the house, at midday I used to go and sit or have a little sleep in the front of San Gwann Church, which was at the top of their road, and the breeze and the cool air was unbelievable, really a big change.

One day I was on the roof with Uncle Mikael when he noticed a soldier pinching some grapes from one of the fields. I have never seen anybody move so fast. He ran towards the top of the yard behind the garage, climbed the wall like a lizard and out of the back door into the field and started running towards the intruder, who ran away as soon as he saw my uncle. He did not have to run far because the army area was only was about 300 metres from the farmhouse and went all the way to the army barracks. The army had a high tower with a clock on the four sides, which was very handy for my mum's family because when they were in the fields, they could see the time. My uncle Beru used to go and buy lots of food from the kitchen staff.

As the afternoon unfortunately arrived, and it was time to think of going back, my aunt Cheleste started discussing with my mum what we were going to take back with us. As my aunt piled up the stuff, my mother kept reminding her that we had a long way to carry it, so the time came to leave, and as we started on the long walk back, I began to think about my next visit. It was not long before I started to moan about carrying my load, but I had to grin and bear it, as they say, anyway it was another visit that I enjoyed.

CHAPTER 16

OUT OF CONTROL

I started very early in life with picking a fight, burning the mattress in the shelters, pinching apricots in school, and upsetting the teacher quite often.

I started after the war, let's say when I was 11 years old, and finished when I left school at 14 and started work, because it will give you some idea of the age I was doing these things.

As I said before, none of the children had anything to keep them indoors, so it was like what we see today in futuristic films with people climbing out of holes in the ground, the only thing we used came out of houses.

We used to gather in groups near Mensija Bar and discuss what we were going to do – play a game or do something else. One of my friends Chico was brought up without a mother, she died when he was young, so he was kind of homely, and he always used to organise us and tell us to get some sugar, tea, milk, and a big tin. When we all came back, we used to go to a field somewhere, find some water and some wood to start a fire and make the tea. I do not know what we used to drink from, at home we used tins, mostly the tins that the condensed milk came in, so maybe we had some of them; we used to do this some Sundays.

One day we were doing a tin of tea on a slab of concrete where the ammunition dump was, and we were doing a bit of wrestling on the concrete near the tin on the fire. A grown man threw a stone over the wall, hit the tin and spilled the hot water over the slab, so we could not get up quick enough away from the hot water, and I think that was the last time we made tea.

In the summer months when the fruit was ripe, it used to be a bad time for the farmers because we liked to share the fruit with them. So the group that came up with the best peaches or grapes or melons we used to go and get it, so I am going to write a few of my adventures.

I will start with one Tony and me did. There was a farmer not far from us who used to have a lot of peach trees, so we decided to go for it. So the plan was that one would go and pick the peaches and the other keep watch. Tony wanted to go and pick the peaches and I would keep guard. To get to where the peaches were, we had to pass the house where the farmer lived. Anyway, Tony went in the field and started picking the peaches, the farmer came out of his house and started running towards Tony. I started making noises that we agreed before, but Tony was so focused that he did not hear me or the farmer, so the farmer caught him and let him go. For me to get back, I had to go by the house, so I waited for a while and then I started back. As I approached, the door opened and the farmer came out and told me that he had seen the whole thing.

Another time, a big crowd of us decided to go and pinch some figs. As it happens, not far from the peach farmer. It was a field or two from the front of his house, and to get in the field, the dry-stone wall was about two metres high, but when we got on the wall, the field was about four metres down. We hesitated for a couple of minutes, and the thought went through my mind how to get out if the farmer came, by this time some of the boys had jumped, so I jumped as well, and everything went alright. I always remember that day because of that high wall.

A few metres away from Mensija Bar where the band club is today, the man who lived there had a field of peach trees, so every year we used to pinch them. My cousin Emanuel lived next to the farmer and could see the field from his roof, so he suggested that he be the lookout and I go and get the fruit. When I got the fruit, I jumped over his field at the back of his house, and he used to hang a rope down and I climbed using the rope to the top of the roof to eat the peaches. So the farmer decided to get a dog, and he got a German shepherd dog and tied it in the middle of the field. I am afraid that did not stop us, so after that he chopped all the trees down.

My cousin was not afraid to use me as a lookout, so sometimes he used to change the lookout role, and like my father used to do, go and pick sand from Pebbles Beach and ask me to be on a lookout for the police. One evening, a crowd of us were debating what to do, so one of us came up with the idea to jump in this garden that was next to Mensija Bar field because they had some pomegranate trees full of fruit, so we decided to go for it. We went and filled our pockets and inside our shirts, as much as we could carry. When we started eating them, we found that they were not ripe, so we started horsing around with them and throwing them at each other. By the time we finished, the front of Mensija Bar was covered with pomegranates, what a sight and because the owner was a good neighbour, he used to help my mother in the fields, I felt so ashamed when I saw that disgusting sight.

After that disaster for everybody to see, my mother decided to lock the front door and lock me in when I was not going to school. If you think that would stop me, it did not. I don't know if you remember me saying, but behind the house there was my uncle Emanuel's field. It was as if somebody prepared a way out for me to get out of the house because in the back wall there were some holes in the wall and a bar in the wall to hold onto. When I was looking for a way out, I even looked at the back of the two houses next door, but I decided to try behind my house. Remember that the buildings at that time were very high. I managed to get down and I ran through my uncle's field and another field, and I was out on the road and back with my friends.

By this time, I was out of control. My mother used to hit me with the nearest thing she could find, broomsticks, ropes, belts that were left from my father, bits of wood, anything.

One day she was running after me with a broomstick, and I ran and ended up on one of the beds, and as she tried to hit me, I grabbed the broomstick with my legs, and before she knew it, she was lying across me, and her head hit the wall. I remember the bad things as well as the good things.

Sometimes men from the village used to have a quiet word with me to behave because my mother had enough problems without me causing any more.

I remembered people that did good and men that were bad to me. There were a few but I am only going to name two. For example, one of them was my cousin Lino; he was a lot older than me, he was the son of my mother's sister Catherine, the same person who helped us a lot during the war. They lived in Birkirkara where I went to school, so I used to bump into him sometimes and he used to completely ignore me. One day, I met him at the barber, we were sitting next to each other and he never said a word, a grown man, as if he didn't want anybody to know that I was his cousin. A man I used to see sometimes on the way to school. I used to see this man in Birkirkara sometimes on his horse and cart, and sometimes he'd be walking. He always stopped and gave me a penny; in those days, a penny was worth a few sweets. I think he was a friend of my father. I explained to my mother what he looked like and the horse, but my mother did not know who he was. What a difference between the two of them.

One day, me and Tony decided to go swimming and we went to Pebbles Beach. Why we decided to walk all that way, I don't know. So we got swimming and we decided to see how high we could dive, so we went in the British Army area and kept going towards where the rocks were getting higher, and every time the rocks got higher, we dived and moved on to the next higher rock. We were getting near to a spot where it had a bad name and a few English soldiers had drowned because of strong currents, anyway we thought we would try it. The rock was about six metres high, we never thought much about the danger and jumped. As I tried to get to the surface, I found myself struggling, and it seemed to take a long time to surface. Anyway, I made it and my first thought was if Tony made it, so I started looking for him. I was relieved when I saw him. We looked at each other and I realised that he had the same trouble, we looked for a good spot to get out onto the rocks and realised that we were a few metres from where we had jumped from.

We got on the rocks and safety and discussed our experience, which happened to be the same. After that we got dressed and were happy to be going home safely.

One day, myself, my brother John, and my friend Pino, the same boy that we found the bones in the niche, went to try to catch some robins. What we used to do was put a robin in a cage trap and put the trap near a tree so we could hide. If there was a robin locally, it would think that another robin was in his territory and it would attack our one and, hopefully for us, it would get caught in the trap. Luckily for the robins, we did not catch any. I remember spending a long time telling Pino about me going to Canada and the crossing over to America. I remember we went to Weid Oliqa, which today is a nature reserve.

On the way back, being upset because we did not catch any robins, we were looking for some mischief. We were passing by a house where one of the rooms had a low roof, so one of us grabbed a stone and threw it on the roof. As soon we got home, there was a knock on the front door and when my mother opened the door, there was the woman of the house we threw the stone on. In her apron, she had the stone we used, and she was telling my mother what we had done. I think she told my mother a lie because she told her we broke one of the stones the roof was made of, and looking at the stone, it was not big enough to break the stone the roof was made of, and she demanded compensation. But my mother told her to go and see the other mother because Pino was older than us so he was responsible and she went away talking to herself.

My best friend Julian used go to a quarry at Tal Ballal, and he told me about some rabbits the owner used to keep in one of the rooms. So, discussing it with another friend Victor, we thought that we could get two and cook them and take them to the sea and have some sort of a picnic.

Victor was quick to say he would get the fat and the saucepan so it was agreed, all we wanted was the rabbits. So, one evening we went to the quarry to get the rabbits, as we were treading softly we heard a noise in one of the rooms, so we went back a bit and stopped to see if we heard any more noises. It was not long before Julian realised that there was a donkey in one of the rooms, so we had a bit of a laugh and carried on with the job.

We got near Victor's house, found a carob tree and some wood and started a fire. The saucepan we had was quite deep so we put the rabbits in, and they fitted in well. Real gourmet cooking, we virtually boiled them in cooking fat but they tasted so good. Victor suggested he take it home and bring it back in the morning.

We met next morning. Victor brought the rabbits and we were off to St Julian to have a swim and a picnic. We had our swim and got the dish, and when we took the cover off, half of the rabbits were missing. I did not say anything and Julian was so hungry he did not notice. I kept wondering why Victor was so industrious all the time.

One afternoon, me and Julian Grima were by Mensija Bar and Spiro was driving by and stopped and told us that he was going to pick up some stuff from a quarry in Tal Ballal and if we wanted to go for a ride, so we said yes and off we went.

When we arrived, Spiro got on with his job and we went to have a look around. It was not long before we saw a grapevine, but unfortunately there were no grapes on it, so now we got the idea to look around for some grapes. We didn't find any, so we crossed the road and got up a two-metre-high dry-stone wall, and when we looked, there were the grapes waiting for us. About a metre and a half away from the wall, there was a well full of water with some arches going across, no roof, and the field made into squares so it was easy to be watered that morning. Anyway, as soon as we jumped in, the farmer appeared on the wall holding a stone to throw at us, shouting his head off. I quickly saw my escape route across the field and towards the road home, so I jumped over the arches over the well and across the wet field down to my ankles in mud when I saw Julian running along the wall, shouting, 'Mother, Mother.' So I asked him to come my way but he kept running until he decided to climb up the wall and, of course, the farmer was waiting for him. He grabbed Julian by his hair, pulled him off the top of the wall and threatened him with the stone. I went a bit nearer, hoping the farmer would come and chase me and leave Julian alone. In the meantime, Spiro had heard what was going on and went to rescue Julian and the farmer let him go, so I kept running towards the way home. As I got to an alley coming off the main road, I had to put the brakes on because I nearly jumped on a horse that died that morning. I stayed there until Spiro picked me up, making sure the farmer was not coming to get me because I had done a lot of damage running across the wet field. After a while, Spiro arrived laughing as he picked me up and dropped us back.

The day after that, Julian told me that he wet the bed and his mother wanted to know what was wrong, but he did not tell her. Julian was two years older than me, so I was surprised how scared he was. This went on for over two weeks, and according to him, he never told his mother. This story I am not very proud of, but it's got to be told to show what we used to get up to because we did not have the things the young boys have today. It doesn't mean you have to be bad, but anything for a laugh or a challenge will do.

In Mensija Road lived a woman on her own in a farm, she was a bit mysterious, and the word was that she had a ghost in the house.

The house had a front door with a big keyhole, and the door led to a big yard full of animals, so when you looked through the keyhole, you could see well into the yard. Sometimes things did not look right, sometimes we saw a man dressed like a Turk just standing in the middle of the yard, so we ran like hell. We used to do anything to torment her. Unfortunately for her, the bigger boys used to torment her as well, only a lot worse than us.

One late morning, a crowd of us were by Mensija Bar, and a big lorry with Coca-Cola signs all over it pulled in front of the bar and the driver called us and gave us a bottle each. It tasted very nice. I don't remember what date it was, I don't think it was much after the war. After that, sometimes a dog full of nits came and hung around the bar, and the owner used to give us a bottle of Coke to get rid of it, so we took it to a deserted field and killed it. Because I never had any money, that was the only way I could get a Coke.

Where the ammunition dump was, they started dumping rubbish, so a lot of stray dogs and cats used to go there to find something to eat. A friend of mine Joseph's father had two dogs, and I think they had some bulldog blood in them because when we took them to the tip, my friend used to let them loose and they chased all the other dogs, and we used to do that quite often.

Talking about fighting dogs. After the war ended, Fort Tal Qroqq was dismantled and abandoned, so it was the ideal place to do something illegal like dog fights.

I don't know what age I was, but I remember going there once or twice. I don't know how they let a boy in,

I think I went with Spiro and his father. We got to this big area full of men, a lot of fierce-looking dogs and a lot of money changing hands. I suppose it was gambling money.

When the dogs started fighting, it was not very nice to watch because one dog used to bite some part of the other dog and didn't let it go until the poor dog's owner gave up, and of course if he gave up and the dog lost, the owner and all the people who backed it lost the money.

It is unbelievable that it is still going on today in England and all over the world because in the world that I grew up in life, as you have read, was a lot harder and more cruel in all different ways than it is today. My mother tried to have a cat to catch mice and maybe rats, but for some reason, I don't know why, I did not like cats, so every time my mother got a cat, I used to get rid of it in a cruel way. Talking of rats, in summer, in the evening, we used to sit in the small yard and sometimes we would see a row of rats coming from the roof, going down the grapevine to the bottom. While writing this book, the question came to my mind, what used to happen to them? Because I don't remember my mother doing anything about it, must have been another ghost site.

One time my mother had 18 chickens at the point of laying eggs, and one morning when she went to feed them, they were all dead, killed by rats. So we found the hole they had come from and I blocked it with cement and bits of glass and set out to find the rats. I still had Brimbo the dog at the time, and he traced them to a heap of straw we had in a corner of one of the animal rooms. So with some tools ready to kill them, we started to clear the straw slowly, and a rat came out and we managed to kill it and the dog helped as well by killing more. Then one of the rats ran up the yard door trying to get out and it got up about two metres, jumped back, and landed on my mother's chest and jumped down again.

One must have got out of the room because I remember I caught up with it in another room. Their hole was blocked but there was a hole in the ground where I had dug to find the hole in the wall, and that's where I caught the rat with the tool I had that had steel at the end of it. With the dog barking its head off, I kept squeezing the rat with the steel end and it tried to bite the steel. I can still hear its teeth crunching on the steel today, and it took a long time for it to die. Ever since that day, I have hated rats.

During the war, the British Army brought Shire horses to Malta. To me, they were a lot bigger than the horses I was used to and very nice. After the war, the people that owned the quarries bought them and made these huge carts and used them to carry the stones from the quarries to the building sites, and as I mentioned before, San Gwann was between Tal Ballal and Sliema, so all day long we had horses going up and down Naxxar Road.

Because I loved horses, I used to admire them all day, and I loved the carts; they were made different to other carts made in Malta, the lengths of wood that went each side of the horse were sort of bent to fit the horse. Years after, I visited Malta with my wife and children, and we visited the lime museum in Siggiewi, which is in a quarry, as it is all related to stones and quarries, but unfortunately they did not have one of these carts. I happened to have a word with the owner and he told me that he could not find one to buy anywhere, which surprised me because Siggiewi was also full of quarries.

Me and Tony heard about a field in New Swieqi full of ripe melons. Because it was near St George's Bay, we thought we go get the melons and go to the sea and eat them by the sea. We met about midday and started towards New Swieqi. We got to the field, looked over the wall, and there was a field full of melons, ripe and ready to be picked. So we looked around to see if there was any problem. Well, there was a shotgun, the farmer was lying in a make-do shelter at the edge of the next field, which was about a metre higher, the farmer was lying with a shotgun next to him. We stopped to think and we made a bit of noise to see if he could hear us, and when there was no movement, we decided to go in. When we picked the melons, we wanted and put them together on the floor, and all the time we kept our eyes on the farmer. But luckily, he must have been having a good sleep because he did not move. So we looked at each other and the question was how were we going to carry the melons? So we looked around, and in the corner near a building there was a donkey happily eating from a sack hanging from its head. So one of us went and took the sack off the donkey, emptied the hay and put the melons in the sack and got out as quick as we could. Luckily for us, the farmer never heard anything.

We got to the seaside all proud of ourselves, and we put the melons in the sea to cool down. There were some older boys next to us who started nosing around and when they saw the melons, asked us for some. Of course, we refused but we had an idea what was likely to happen but there was nothing we could do; there were four or five of them and a lot older than us.

Wenzu came up with the idea to swim with the melons across the bay to where the British Army were, even though he knew that once he get there the soldiers would chase him off. We knew because we used to cross over to jump from their boards and they would come after us, pointing their guns until we jumped in the sea and swam across to our side. He would not listen to me, so he grabbed the sack and went in the sea to start to swim across. As soon as the boys saw that, they jumped and soon caught him up – with the heavy melons, he had no chance. They took the melons and gave us one back. When I got home, my mother had already heard what I had done and grabbed something to hit me with. How she heard about it was that a farmer across the valley called Marion had seen us and he recognised me because my uncles had fields near there and must have seen me with them. Another bad day for my poor mother.

Near Ta Grezju field there was a big scrapyard, so Tony and me and Victor decided to go and pinch some lead. Victor said he could sell it. So one evening, me and Tony carrying guns went to pinch some lead. We went in the yard and picked up as much lead as we could carry; we had to carry the stuff over some dry-stone walls to get to Victor's house.

The next day, Victor sold the lead, and because we only got a little money, we decided it was not worth doing it again.

I learned a lot at an incredibly young age, some very helpful, some very hurtful. Like when I was very young, a man from the village told me that my father owed him 13 shillings that day. So, I went and told my mother, and my mother went and threw the money at him.

Another hurtful lesson I learned. I was playing with some older boys, and my mother came and told the boys not to encourage me to do bad things, one of the boys told her to control her son and not tell them what to do. Unfortunately, I learned that he was right that you have to put your house in order before you tell others what to do.

Before I carry on with my story, I will tell you some of the stories I grew up with. In the evenings, my mum and the neighbours used to get together and talk all night, before I tell you what sort of conversation they had, I will tell you about them. These were people that were born just before 1900 or just after; they lived mostly by nature, by watching the sun, the moon and what the weather told them, by superstition, and by information that passed from father to son and mother to daughter. But although they were not educated, they were not stupid. Some of them generated money and raised families like my grandfathers. Like my uncle Gamri, one of the children just sold his inheritance for one and half million euros, like my uncle Bertu when he died it was found that he had investments in England in the post office and in some companies which I sorted out. Unfortunately, the companies went bankrupt but I found some money in the post office account.

They used to start by saying the rosary and they used to talk about farming, some gossip of the day and some stories of the past. They used to tell stories about ghosts, and I would like to tell you now that to a lot of Maltese people, ghosts existed, and a lot of people had their own experience, like my family had their own experience.

In San Gwann Church, the first Mass used to be very early. One morning, the woman that lived across the road knocked on the door and told my mother not to go to the Mass because on the way to the church, there was a man dressed in black standing by a gate, and she returned home.

A lot of people saw this man within 20 metres of my house. One story they talked about was a man in San Gwann who had a Karozzin, a horse cab, he used to work in Sliema and he worked till the early hours of the morning. One morning when he was going home, he heard a baby crying, so he picked it up and took it home, but when he got home, the baby told the man to take it back so he did.

They believed a lot of stories. Like a man in Rabat that he'd seen this pig in the house and followed it to the basement and it disappeared into a wall, so the man opened the wall and he found a lot of gold sovereigns. They also believed that they appeared because there was money hidden, or somebody got murdered, somebody left money to the church and the church abandoned the person. Like we believed what happened in our house because when we had problems, my mother used to offer a couple of masses to the person and the problem used to stop, like the house that frightened the horse. The saying was that some men were playing cards, had an argument and one got killed.

They used to say that the ghost only had four fingers and no thumb, so it could not strangle you. They talked about a farmer in our village, and that the ghost gave him a lot of money and he told some friends, and when he went back to his farm the ghost gave him a good beating and he never went back.

I could keep going on writing, but if you don't believe in ghosts, it might get a bit boring, but while I am writing, the hair at the back of my neck feels funny.

They used to discuss when to sow the crops, and I remember one night they were discussing whether it was the right time to put the chicken on the eggs and started talking about whether the moon was in the right position or something. I do not know what they used the moon for, whether it was for fertility or the date, because they did not have any calendars or watches, but they used to discuss the moon even when they were sowing crops.

They used to talk about what the bible predicted and that people would be doing all sorts of things.

They talked about things that happened in the past such as when there was a big wind tunnel, and it picked up a man who was on a thrashing pit and dropped him about two kilometres away, and of course a lot more, but it was a long time ago and I don't remember.

CHAPTER 17

WORKING AFTER SCHOOL

My uncle Manwel got me a job with his friend's son who was a floor-tile layer; the job was in a big block of flats in Gzira. Working on a big building site with men and a lot going on was not easy, there were no stairs to go to the upper floors; the only way to go up there was a platform that went up and down on a guide. The platform was about one and half metres by one metre, and no safety rail surrounded it, so it was a bit scary. I also had to take the tiles and cement on the platform, and when it stopped at the top, it used to shake a lot and I used to be very worried. The builders used to use a hoist to take the stones to the upper floors with an improvised lorry, they jacked the lorry on stones, took the tyre off one of the wheels, put wire rope in the rim and made a hoist out of it.

The worst thing about the job was the tiles we used were only made a few days before and the cement was still fresh, and I had to use my hands without gloves. After a little while, the tips of my fingers started bleeding, and the only way I could make the tips of my fingers harder was by weeing on them and all over my hands; very unhygienic, but it was the remedy. After a few months, the job come to an end and the man did not have a job to go to, so he put me off.

Luckily, I got a job on the same building with Vincent, a glazer, he had the job of doing the whole block, so I started taking the glass up to him, and I was up and down on the platform again.

When I was in front with the glass, I started installing the glass myself and I was faster than him, so he became the labourer and I did that for the rest of the job.

While I was doing that, the builder was finished and the time came to seal the roof. So about six women arrived one morning, got on the platform, and with all the men whistling, were taken onto the roof. They spread the wet, very fine broken pottery and spent all day long smoothing it till it was perfect, singing Maltese folklore all day.

When the glass job finished, Vincent and I got a job with the main contractor. My first job was with a man to do the safety surround on the balconies. When we finished them, the foreman started giving me jobs on my own. On top of the toilets they had a small cupboard, and on the outside wall they left it open, so I had to go in lying down and put louvres to close the gap. Because I was claustrophobic sometimes, I pushed myself out as fast as I could. Another job I remember doing was to go up on what was called a bozen chair that hung from ropes. I had to sit on it and pull myself up six floors and paint the same louvres. While I was doing that, I had a younger boy helping me, that's how I remember because while I was high, I wanted some help and he fell asleep, and I had to shout until somebody else heard me.

Because there were a lot of boys working on site, every lunchtime we used to find an empty room and do some wrestling or play football.

The job came to an end, but you can still see my work of 70 years ago, the building is at the bottom of Gzira Hill in front of the police station.

After the job finished, the company gave me a messenger job in their office, and there I met the owners of the company. One was a colonel in the Maltese army, he came from a very famous family, one was a captain in the Maltese army, not a very nice person, the other one was a Mr Bell, a Scottish navy commander. I did not see much of the colonel because he had his own office in the main street. The office was at the end of Strait Street, the other end was famous for brothels often visited by British sailors. The office consisted of three rooms; one had two clerks and me, and the two others were for the governors. Next door was a perfume importer, and his messenger was a boy called Manwel; we got on very well, and because he had been doing the job for a while, he helped me with the addresses.

The job was handy because when a new film came out, I used to see it at lunchtime.

One day, I made some sort of a bomb with cordy, remember, and I hung it on Manwel's belt at the back and lit it. Of course, Manwel ran and slipped on the floor tiles, luckily he did not get hurt.

While I was working in the office, Mr Bell moved into a new house and asked me to go to his house some mornings and do his garden. He had a very old house called Quarena Palace in Qrendi; about five years ago, Brad Pitt stayed there while in Malta making a film. Mr Bell was doing some work in his house and I used to interpret for him with the workers. One of the things they did was because there was no tap water and he used the water from the well, so the builders put two water tanks close to the ceiling in the kitchen, connected a water pump from the well, and that became the running water. I will come to the tanks later. The other job I remember the builders doing was painting the doors upstairs. One day the owner came and when he saw the doors painted, he started crying because the paintings on the doors were very old, and he thought they were ruined, but the owner took them and had them restored.

Mr Bell had a butler, an old man called Fred who was an ex-navy man. Mr Bell had a party, which the house was suited for – you go through the front door into a big hall with a ceiling two stories high, and upstairs around the hall there was a passage going round with rooms coming from it. Fred and myself used to help with the drinks, and Fred used to cook some eggs if the guest asked for them. They were very generous when we gave them a drink, they always offered us one; Fred used to drink it and I used to pour it into the nearest flowerpot. One day we could smell a big stink in the kitchen, and when I investigated, I found rats drowned in the water tanks Mr Bell used for drinking and cooking, so he got the builders to clean them and put a cover over them.

Quarena Palace

One August day, Mr Bell asked me when I finished his garden to go to the captain's house to do a bit of his garden. I arrived about midday in the boiling sun and the garden was full of dried sunflower plants, so I started to take the plants out, and after a while, I wanted a drink, so I knocked on the garden door and asked the servant for a glass of water, finished the job and went to the office.

The next morning, the captain came in and right away he started shouting at Mr Bell that I woke him up when he was asleep and how useless I was. Mr Bell got fed up and told him that he was happy with me and not to use me again. That was the first time that I came against tribalism; he did not like me because I did not come from his town.

Going back to the parties. Mr Bell told me he had a party coming and he wanted me to find a man in Qrendi who owned a donkey and was prepared to bring the donkey to the party because he wanted to use it. So I found a man and I told him that he would probably be at the party into the early morning, and he was OK with that.

The party started and the man let me know that he had arrived about nine. I gave him a drink and told him to wait, and I would let him know when he was needed. At 11, I went to see him, and he was getting fed up. I told him I would let Mr Bell know, and Mr Bell told me the guests had not had enough to drink yet.

Time went on. I kept the man happy with drinks, and at one in the morning, Mr Bell asked me to bring the donkey. I went to tell the man, who by now was furious and started shouting that he wanted more money. I cooled him down and told him that he would be happy with the money and went in to wait for instructions. Mr Bell and a young woman came near the donkey, the music started playing 'Streets of Laredo', and the lady was helped to get on the donkey. Mr Bell walked the donkey around the hall while the music played.

When the music finished, I paid the farmer and because I told Mr Bell that he kept moaning, he gave him a good tip.

The party carried on for ever and everyone was enjoying themselves. By this time some had gone upstairs, so we were serving drinks up there. As I was going upstairs, Fred appeared on top of the stairs, and as he started to tell me that he was drunk, he fell and landed in front of me with his face bleeding all over. Everybody gathered, some came out of their rooms half-dressed trying to help Fred, but apart from his face he was alright. I waited for the buses to start in the morning to take him to his home in Hamrun. When his wife opened the door and saw his face, she started shouting, 'You have been drunk again,' so I made a quick exit.

Not long after that, Mr Bell moved to a house next to a big place that used to be a wine-making place. The company bought it to start making furniture, so they had to do some alterations and sometimes I worked there. One job I remember doing was when they bought a load of planks from St Georges square in Valletta where there was a function or something and they surrounded the square with a fence for security, so I had to travel with the lorry for security. Even at that young age, they gave me responsible jobs.

I was still working in the office part time, and one day they told me to take some money to a lawyer at the other end of Strait Street, which meant I had to pass where the brothels were. As I was walking by one bar, there were two women standing by the door and started chatting me up. Before I knew it, with one pulling and one pushing, I was upstairs. I was mostly worried about the money because even at 15 or 16, I was not worried about the women. We sat round a table, they had their bit of fun, and I left happily to deliver the money.

I had to deliver letters and parcels all over Malta. One place I used to go to quite often was the dockyards, and that is where I met the first feadfaile, or gay man, call him what you want, but I got wise to him very quickly. I won't say I encouraged him, but I knew what he was up to and I could handle him. I felt comfortable, but he thought he was getting somewhere. When I stopped being a messenger, I did not see him any more until one day I met him in St. Julian's. He asked me to go for a drink and he was worse than ever, and of course I enjoyed it, especially when I told him that I was going to emigrate. He got so mixed up he spilled a glass of beer all over him and that cooled him down, and I left him there gazing into fresh air.

I got to know a bit about the company. They had about five jobs in Malta, they also had a big job in Bengasi Libya, and we used to send men to work there. The wives used to come to the office for the clerks to write a letter to their husbands, but they did not like doing it, so they used to ask me to write them. One letter I remember well; one woman wrote to her husband and told him to come back as soon as he could. He came back, and the next day he stabbed the leader of the Labour Party, luckily in the arm, and the leader of the Labour Party resigned the next day and they elected Mr Mintoff.

When I was about 17, I started to go to work in a big block of flats in Sliema in the morning, and the afternoon in the office.

I don't remember what I did but I always got my own job. One job I remember doing was that I used to hang on a long plank on two ropes from six floors (20 metres) high, painting the wall.

Remember Tony the bitch that I mentioned before? He was not a very nice man, so the men used to give him a bit of grief. They used to throw paper full of cement mix at him when they could, he started blaming me even in the afternoon when the other men told him that I was not there.

One day I was working in a room upstairs when Tony appeared through the door holding a penknife and raving and shouting that he was going to kill me. There I was, facing a furious man all alone. I started thinking how I could protect myself, so I started going backwards into a door behind me, and he kept coming forwards. As I entered the room backwards, to my right there was a steel bar leaning against the wall, about a metre long. What a relief, I had found something to defend myself with, so I grabbed the bar and now I started going forward, telling Tony to try to kill me now. At that moment, Vince appeared behind him and he told Tony to go away.

I think the manager heard about it, and the next day Tony was paid off.

On the site, there were two brothers working as plumbers: one was Salvu, short for Salvatore, and some days they used to start singing Neapolitan songs. I think they used to sing in public in the evening and they were very good singers. When they finished, I used to have a go, and everybody started shouting for me to shut up.

Salvu was nice, and he used to tell me to go and learn how to sing.

Vince told me that he was trying to get the glass contract and he asked me to be his partner, so I thought I could save some money for when I emigrate. We got the contract, and I left the office job and started with the glass job. One weekend on and a big boil appeared on the thumb on my right hand, so I could not go to work. I went to tell Vince about it and I went home. On the Tuesday, I began to feel desperate so I told my mother that I was going to cut it off. She did not like the idea at all but by the afternoon I decided to cut it off, so I got a new razor blade and cut it. I still have the scar today, all the gunge came out, and the next day I went back to work.

When the job finished, I got a job with the same company as before. By this time, some of the flats were finished and it was time to hand them to the British forces, the owners, so their rep used to come and inspect them before the handover.

I got the job to go with him round the flats and he told me what to put right. I had a big corner in a room in a finished flat full of different things, wood, wall paint, my tools, and everything that I was likely to need.

When the job finished, to my surprise at just 18, I was promoted as a foreman in charge of refurbishing the Mosta football ground.

I met Mr Bell on site and he explained to me about the job, and that next morning the men and some tools were arriving, but we needed some more men, and if any man came that looked all right, I was to tell him the rate of pay and employ him.

An old boy asked about a job, and I asked him how old he was and what he did. He told me he was 70 and a miner, and because it was summer I asked him if he would be all right in that heat, and he said he would be, so I gave him a job. After he told us that he had just returned from America, that gave the boys some excuse to gee him up all day about how stupid he was to come to work in the hot sun.

Although we only used hand tools, the job progressed well, so it was time to bring in tradesmen to do the finishing, one old man to level the ground and one man to build the dry walls around the ground. The captain also sent his brother Carmel to be in charge. He was an old man, half dead, and all he did was sit under a carob tree writing letters to his German girlfriend.

One side of the pitch we had a carob tree, and on the other side I had a room above another, which I used as an office, and went there because, with the door and the window open, I used to get a nice breeze to cool the hot sun.

When the man came to build the dry wall, he spoke to Carmel, so he got involved. They discussed the wall and the builder stretched the line only about 20 metres long, so I told him he should stretch the line all the way, and he suggested I go and tell Carmel so I did. He told me I was only in charge of the pitch. When the builder stretched the line for the second bit of wall, it did not look right so I pointed it out to the builder and told him that it was going to look bad on him if the wall was not straight. I walked away and left it to him with me watching from a distance. He called Carmel and when he told him, Carmel shouted, 'Where is that pregnant woman?' and called me and told me to sort it out, and he disappeared under the carob tree. We had to cut a lot of rocks and we used dynamite, but because I did not know about explosives, one was perfect, and with the other, the debris flew sky-high. Can you imagine an eighteen-year-old using dynamite today?

The old man that came used old ways to level the pitch. At that time the pitch was hard, and it had to be high in the middle and ramped towards the sides, so when it rained the water went to the side. I asked how he was going to do it, and he said, 'I get a length of wood, and every length I go down the height of a box of matches,' and that's how he did it.

One late morning I was in my office doing some paperwork when one of the workers came running in. He ran behind me, shouting, 'Fred is going to kill me.'

A few seconds after, Fred came through the door brandishing a big knife, shouting, 'I am going to kill you.' So I stood up and told him to stop this. Fred was one of the captain's spies and I did not like him and he knew it, so my thinking was that he might just stick the knife in me as well. Within my mind, I looked for something to protect myself, and the man would not calm down, but after a lot of worry I calmed him down.

Because it was summer and very hot, I had a boy of 16 go round with a tin full of water giving the men a drink. I always thought that he was gay, and one day he came in my office and tried to get fruity with me, so I grabbed the tin and threw the water all over him and that cooled him down.

I was coming to the end of the job, so I started to finish men off for the first time, which was not a nice thing to do. The first man I started with was Fred. I did not mind giving him his cards because he told the captain what was happening on the job, so when I was giving his cards, I told him, 'This is for spying on me,' and a tear came out of his eyes.

Mr Bell was happy with the job and sorry that I was emigrating and told me that if ever I came back, he would always have a job for me.

MOSTA'S NEW FOOTBALL GROUND
Levelling Work Nearing Completion
By BROTHER CUTHMAN,
Secretary, Malta Playing Fields Association.

To many the Mosta Football Ground is reminiscent of neglect and winter mud baths; for those plucky youngsters who, in winter time, risked their neck on the slippery surface only one thing was good enough: to renew the ground completely.

Levelling work in progress at Mosta's new football ground.

Mosta Football Ground: I am the last one on the left.

While I was working in Mosta, my mother asked if me and John could dig a well before I emigrated. I said yes but John and I were not so keen because it was a big job. We started digging with hand tools because there were no jack hammers in those days, we found the rocks were very hard because the rocks in Malta were so different, and we happened to find one of the hardest, and the deeper we got, the harder it got. John kept complaining and I kept seeing him up and that was an excuse for him to go up and leave me to it. When we had a load of rocks, Spiro used to clear it for us with his lorry.

At the time, I was using dynamite in Mosta, so I thought I would use it in the well. Of course, it was in a building area and I was not experienced. I never told my mother, so I had a trial and I asked Marie if she could hear any noise, and she said no, so I was happy to carry on using the dynamite, which made life a lot easier. We eventually got to the bottom about six metres deep, and my mum was happy.

A Well similar to the one I dug

CHAPTER 18

MY GROWING YEARS AT FOURTEEN

I began by telling you how I saw the problem my mother had with my uncles as a fourteen-year-old. Seeing my mother going through that trauma with three big men with nobody to help her and me feeling so helpless.

After my uncles scared my mother in the field, I decided to do something about it, so I remembered my friend, the gun, and I said to myself, *When the opportunity arrives, I will shoot the three of them*. One afternoon a meeting was arranged between the four of them at my mother's lawyer's office, so I thought that was a good time for me to find them together. Luckily, my guardian angel came to my rescue and the meeting was cancelled.

But I did not stop hating them, and after a lot of arguments, it was settled and we inherited a house and a field in New Swieqi. So it was time to move to the new house. My father built a room in the old house for the animals, and because the problems my mother got from my uncles, she told me to take it down. But because it showed on the plans, it had to stay, so me and John had to build it again. Thinking about it now, I don't know how my mother could ask 14 and 12-year-old kids to build a room with those heavy stones and no experience at all. I do not remember much about the dismantling or of the building of the room, but I think I remember about it because of the lintel on the door. It was not very long but it was a rough stone, normally stones are 200 by 275mm and any length, but this beam was about 400 round and I had to put it on top of the doorway. I remember putting one side up and the struggle to put the other side up, and it's the only thing that stuck in my mind. I don't remember how I took the stones up. I don't remember how I did the roof; I only remember the beam over the door because it was such a struggle. After that, we moved across the road to the new modern house, not only one toilet but two and a bathroom.

Because the field in Swieqi belonged to us, my mother wanted to make it as fertile as possible and that meant hard work. The farmers used a method called pyramids, which means you stand still and pull the ground towards you with a tool we called wide masqa – sometimes you see them in Egyptian documentaries – over your feet and forming a trench about 900mm wide and 250mm deep. So by this time, you've got a pyramid around your feet; it was backbreaking.

It was a bit long to travel and before long, my mother planted grapevines all over it, and that saved us a lot of work.

We had nothing to do with my father's family after we moved to the new house because we never forgot how badly they treated us.

By now, John had started work and my mother opened the shop, so we gave the fields up and life went on. By this time, I had started work in the office, which meant it was a bit strange because I was the only person in San Gwann going to work dressed for office work.

One day I was coming home, and as I was passing my aunt Ganna she said something sarcastic about the way I was dressed. By this time, I could face anybody so I saw the opportunity to do what I had wanted to do a few months earlier. So I went in, got the gun, got out in the road, and I challenged Ganna's husband, Wenzu, to come out and answer for his wife's remarks so I could burn him out. When the neighbours heard me say that, they came out but there was no sign of Ganna or Wenzu, and I never spoke to any of them before I left for England.

As I was growing up, I made a lot of friends with football fans, farmers, builders and shop keepers, and I had friends older than me, which was good because some of them had cars. I seem to make friends with a lot of different guys.

Sometimes a crowd of us used to go to the seaside on a lorry that belonged to a guy that had cows, and the back of the lorry used to be packed.

One day we went to Paradise Bay. We used to like it there because there was a small sandy beach and some high rocks we used to jump from. One day as we arrived by the rocks, we disturbed a nest of sparrows and one flew and fell in the sea, so I decided to try and rescue it and I swam towards it. The boys were directing me towards the bird because they could see it from high on the rocks, it seemed further and further away, and at the end I got the bird, and swimming back with one hand above water was not easy, and that was the third time I had to struggle with the sea.

One day we decided to go to Gozo. I was about 16, and it was the first time for me and a few others to go to Gozo, so I went to help Joseph, the man who owned the truck, to clean it ready for an early start the next day. With a truck full of young and older boys, we made our way to the ferry, we got to Gozo and headed for the beach, had a good swim and it was time for lunch.

By now we were in holiday mood and looking for a good meal and maybe a glass or two of wine. Most of the restaurants are by the sea, but for some reason we ended up in one in a village. We sat down, and nobody looked at the menu because we looked forward to a rabbit meal before we went.

We had a fair drink of wine and when we finished the meal, we crossed the narrow road and fell asleep on the pavement.

We got up about two hours later and headed for the ferry and back to San Gwann. One of the boys on the outing was my friend Julian. We liked Gozo a lot and we started going there often. We used to look at the hills and say they'd make good scenery for cowboy films because me and Julian used to rush to see every cowboy film as soon as it started showing. Julian used to give every film star a nickname; our favourite film was *Streets of Laredo*.

Because I liked cowboy films so much, I decided to make a cowboy suit. I bought a shirt an old man had and this big hat. It was dirty and torn but I thought I could make it look good, so I asked him if he'd give it to me, and he took it off and handed it to me. I ran home and washed it and left it to dry.

I asked my mother for a length of white ribbon and sewed it round the rim of the hat, which made it look good. Next, I wanted a gun belt, so I made one. Now I was ready for the carnival and to have some photos taken, so me and my friend started to take photos very often.

Next thing I got interested in was folk music and folk singing, and I used to go where they used to meet. One evening, two young guys used to come to San Gwann and play the guitar, all single chords, and I liked the music a lot.

I also liked the marching bands that played in the feasts, so I decided to join the band of St Julian. I went to see the headmaster, and when I told him I wanted to play the trumpet, he said I wouldn't be able to play it because my lips were too big, so I said trumpet or nothing, so he agreed for me to try.

After weeks of practising with my hands to get the rhythm, I got the trumpet, so then I got to do lots of practice and that sent my mum mental. I was doing very well, and I was on the edge of starting to play in the feast, but it was time to emigrate.

In the meantime, I was learning to play the guitar and the guy that used to teach me was the brother of the guy that was teaching the trumpet. I liked the guitar, and I was beginning to play songs in single chords; my favourite song was 'Verde Luna', a Spanish song.

I played once in public with my teacher and another guy in a very crowded bar in St Julian's, and the occasion was to celebrate Queen Elizabeth's coronation because it was on the day.

Before I emigrated, I thought I had better get a driving licence, so I asked Julian Brifa if he could teach me to drive. He agreed, so we hired a car, went into the country, and as I started to drive, he started to shout at me for driving too fast. We hired a car every Saturday or Sunday until it was time to go for a driving test, and I passed the first time.

CHAPTER 19

CONCLUSION

Writing these few lines raises more questions than answers. Was I trying to compete with other boys or trying to be better than the boys that had older brothers and fathers to help them? Is that why I was always ready to accept a challenge, such as going out of my street knowing that I could be in a fight at any time, with all the big boys encouraging the other boys.

What made me risk my life pinching a few melons with a farmer 10 metres away with a shotgun ready to blast me off?

Building a room at 14 years old with the big stones, and facing the biggest challenge of my life lifting the lintel above the door. When I lifted near the top, and I couldn't lift it any higher, but the choice I had was to take it up or let it fall on top of me, so I had to find extra strength from somewhere, and thank God I did, and that was the first time I was near to crying because of the problem I was in.

Now it was time to go to England, and because of the life I lived and the things that I went through, I think I was prepared for whatever came my way, like bullying, racism and whatever the world we live in could offer. All my friends wanted to see me off at the airport but because it was a working day only 12 of them could make it.

I stopped my mother from coming to the airport because when I worked as a messenger, I saw enough people crying when they were seeing their relatives getting on ships going to Australia from Valletta harbour and did not want to go through all that.

I do not remember going to the airport except going down Gzira Hill when we were passing a friend driving a lorry, and I shouted 'goodbye', and he shouted back, 'You are making a big mistake.'

At the airport, I wondered what went on in people's minds when they saw me shaking hands with all the boys. As we were shaking hands, some of them said, 'I will see you in England,' which more than half did. As I got on the plane, I started to wonder whether I would see Malta again, but turned my mind to the future and England and forgot all the things I loved about Malta.

Goodbye Malta.

CHAPTER 20

ARRIVING IN ENGLAND

The plane was a new experience, so I was a bit worried about it, and as it happens, I had reason to because the plane did not have jet engines but propellers, and that meant as we flew along, the plane hit air pockets and dropped down about 40 metres and up again, and that happened all the way to England.

I landed at Heathrow Airport, which in those days was called London Airport, in a strange world and to a new life. I took a taxi as I was advised before I left Malta.

I got in the taxi. It was dark and raining, and I told the taxi driver the address, Wilkes Street, East London, and he told me he didn't know where it was. So then I told him to go to Fashion Street and once and again he said he did know where it was and he gave a small *A to Z* book and told me to look for the streets. As you can imagine, I did not know the first thing about looking in that book. To add to it, it was dark in the cab, and the writing was very small and I could not see anything. Later, I learned that the Wilkes Street address was practically a brothel and could set me on a different path altogether than the one I took.

So, I told the taxi driver a third address, Vallance Road, East London, and right away he said, 'Oh, I know where that is,' so we carried on our way to my friend Spiro who lived at that address.

I did not ask to go to Spiro because he had his family and his brothers-in-law living with him and I did want to be a problem.

I knocked on the door, and as it happened Spiro opened the door, and he was pleased to see me. He called his wife, Teresa, and told her; they made me welcome with a cup of tea and a sandwich and I told them about the other addresses, and Spiro told me all about Wilkes Street. They offered me to stay with them but the only thing that they could offer was to sleep in a bed with his brothers-in-law Freddy and Tony. By now it was getting late, and I did not have much choice, so I accepted until I found something else. Tony had something wrong with his feet, he used to rub them together all night, and Freddy, I think, was a bit gay, although he got married after, so it was different to what I was used to before I came to England. Talk about a new life.

The next morning, I went with my friend Julian to a café in Hackney where there were a few boys that I knew. I asked a few times for one to show me where the post office was so I could send a telegram to my mother to tell her I arrived safely, and Tony passed some sarcastic remark about 'don't rush'. When I heard it, I started walking towards him to hit him but I thought better of it and I stopped, so Julian took me.

After a little while, I went to live in a café. The café was owned by Bill and Rosa, an Italian woman. Bill was a nice person and every morning he used to look in the papers for a job for me.

Looking for a job was different than today. I used to walk up a long road and go to all the places I thought might have a job, and when I had done a long walk, I crossed the road and did the same on the other side of the road. Only most of the time, I was told to fuck off with a wave of an arm.

My main aim was to get a job that paid well. The first job I found was in a big clothes factory, in the storeroom, paying £4.50 a week while I worked there. I kept looking for better-paying jobs, and one job I was promised was collecting broken glass, which means shovelling the glass into lorries, but when I went back to see the owner, he told me that he gave the job to someone else. Spiro and Teresa had a little boy called Joseph, and I became his godfather. When I moved to the café that Bill and Roza owned, I started sharing a room above the café with another guy called Charlie. By this time, four of my friends had come from Malta, and I got them a room in the same place and a job with me as well, by this time I was working in a veneer factory, and my wage was £5 a week.

As I said before, Bill was a nice guy and he and Rosa did not get on very well. I think she treated him very badly, and all she was interested in was boys, me included, and when I saw her ready to cheat on Bill, I did not like her at all, so whenever she got near me, I walked away.

One night, Bill was not very well but Rosa would not go near him. She was very joyful with the boys while Bill was dying upstairs.

In the early hours of the morning, an ambulance arrived, and Bill was taking to hospital where he died of an overdose. That was a big shock to me because although I was not naive, it changed my attitude towards women because of how bad she was to let him die. I think she knew that he took some pills and she enjoyed seeing him die. But because the café was in a good position and a lot of my friends lived there, I stayed living there. We were near two cinemas and I went to see the first film with Julian, *Quo Vadis*. We lived a few metres from the Hackney Empire theatre and we used to go there every week to a new variety show, and I saw some acts that I still remember today.

There was also a fairground, and all fairgrounds were often visited by Teddy boys, so it was inevitable that one night we would have a fight with them.

One night a few of us were in the café having a drink, and about 10 some boys came back, went in through the side door, and went straight upstairs. We thought it was strange that they did not come to say hallo, so one of us went to see what was happening and he did not come down for a long time. So we all went up, and the boys were all looking in mirrors at their bruised faces and they were in a bad state.

Next evening while we were having a drink, we decided to do something about it. So a few nights after, their wounds healed, a group of us went to the fair, grabbed a rifle each or something we could use as weapons, and one of the boys tried to encourage trouble. But for some reason, the Teddy boys did not respond. We left, and on the way we kept a look out for the Teddy boys but they were nowhere to be seen.

I kept changing jobs to increase my wages, maybe by a pound a week. The first Christmas Eve, I worked in a milk dairy on nightshift, outside loading lorries for one guinea, one pound and five pence, which went towards spending time going round St James' Square near Piccadilly with a young lady.

I got a job in a big scrapyard, and I had a terrible job melting the inside of batteries. It was in the time of the

Teddy boys; they had their own hairstyle, the way they dressed, and they loved a fight, and they used anything to fight with. They used to spend all day looking for something to use as knuckledusters.

One of the workers had been in Malta as a soldier and had some trouble with the Maltese and ended up limping, so he made it known that he did not like me. So that gave the Teddy boys reasons to dislike me as well. One was that I was a foreigner, this man stirring them up, and the worst one was the two girls serving in the canteen, who were going out with friends of mine, so when they served me, they filled my plate up, and you can imagine the Teddy boys' faces when they realised that I was getting preferential treatment.

I expected that one day they'd find me in a corner and give me a good hiding, so I thought I would take control, and the place to make it happen was the canteen as maybe somebody would come to my rescue. So I picked my dinner, and as I turned round, the Teddy boys were sitting on this long table, about seven of them, and in the middle of the table there was an empty chair. I thought *now or never,* so I went and sat down, never saying anything, and waiting for the sparks to start. One of the boys sitting opposite me said in a cockney accent, 'Are you Maltese?' and I said yes, and he said, 'I am a Maltese as well,' and that cleared the air, and after a bit of conversation, we were all friends. I was glad that it worked all right, and thanks to Victor, I got away with being a bit brave and the boys accepted that I was not afraid of them.

After that, I got a job in a handbag factory. I was put on a machine cutting the material and I did very well. The workforce was mostly women, there were only four men. One of the boys was a bit proud of himself and he tried to bully me in front of the girls, although he was a lot bigger than me, I was not having it, so I waited for him to go in the toilets and I followed him in. I leaned against the door and I challenged him to have a laugh now. His face started to change colour and he apologised and said he would not do it again. After a few months in England, that was the second time I had to stop being bullied. Before that, he knew what I could do because we used to get the material from the store upstairs and we met there, himself, his mate, and an older man, and the boys started wrestling me. I grabbed one with my legs and I handled the other one with my hands. As the older man had seen it all, he kept on asking me to take up wrestling because it was extremely popular at the time, but I kept refusing because I was not a public person and I thought I was too heavy for my size.

Two of my best friends Julian and Zaren

I was lucky to get my own flat in Aldgate near Brick Lane. I decided to leave the job, and I told the older brother Jack of the two brothers, and he was surprised and walked away to talk to his brother and his father and went to their office. Jack came back and asked me if I wanted any more money. I said that I wanted to work outside. He looked at me and walked away again to speak to his family, and after a few minutes he came back and told me to stop the machine and go with him.

We arrived in this large, empty land except for some scrubs and trees and a large shed. It was near the canal in Mile End, East London, where the university is today.

We walked all the way to the end, and on the way back, he said, 'I am going to build my factory here. Would you like to work here?' and I said yes. He asked if I knew anything about building, and I told him that I worked in building in Malta and that I was a foreman doing the football ground. So we went back to his office and he showed me the drawings and asked me what materials we needed for him to order and whether I knew somebody to give me a hand. So I said yes, and I employed my friend Freddy. We started on a Monday and after breakfast, the architect Mr Green arrived, a man of about 40 years old, a man I found easy to talk to. Jack, the architect and I were discussing the job and before long Mr Green seemed to be talking to me more and more, and Jack did not mind because he did know anything about building, and he was learning as much by listening as talking.

The job was going well, and the tradesmen started coming, and Mr Green would only discuss the job with me. The first trade to arrive was the piling company, Terry Tayler was the foreman, we got on well, and at the end of his job he said if ever I need a job to ask him.

Me and Fred used to go out to a café for breakfast, and we used to amaze everybody by the size of the breakfast; it consisted of a full plate of everything and six slices of thick bread.

After the piling finished, the bricklayers arrived and big lorries full of bricks started arriving, all to be unloaded by hand, no forklifts, and only three of as to unload. I used to sweat a lot and every driver used to ask me if I was OK. The bricks are loaded so they are easy to pick up, so you pick as many bricks as you can handle, but as you lift more and more, it involves strength and experience because you need a lot of skill when the numbers increase.

When we got the first load, the driver was picking about ten and I started picking about six. I started increasing the number and by the end I could lift fourteen, but it was very difficult because when you lift that amount, you had to form a sort of arch; otherwise, the middle would fall.

As the job was going very well, sometimes Jack used to call me into a corner away from everybody and give me some extra money, he really appreciated what I was doing.

We were coming to the end, and Mr Green asked me where my next job was, and I told him that I was going to pack the job in because I did not want to work in a factory. He said that he thought I was a contractor, so he suggested that I start working on my own and he would give me all the work I could handle and help me with all the paperwork. But because I was only 20 years old, I refused and he was very disappointed.

The work finished and Jack offered me a foreman's job in the factory. I told him I wanted a few days off and I would let him know later.

My hair had been falling out for some time, and just before the job was finished, I read that there was a doctor in Blackpool that could treat hair loss, so I bought a ticket to Manchester and off I went. I stayed in Salford and travelled to Blackpool from there. I saw Dr Pye and he gave me some stuff to put on my hair but, unfortunately, I think it was for hair loss and not for hair cure.

So, I came back to my flat in East London. The flat was located near Petticoat Lane, the most famous market in London. There were two sections, one sold all clothes and the other sold everything, tools, dogs, birds, everything you could think of. Some of my friends used to go on a Sunday and afterwards they'd come to my flat for a cup of tea or coffee and, sometimes, we played a game of poker and then go and have lunch in one of the Maltese cafes. When I came back from Blackpool, I started thinking of my next move. I was walking in High Street in Aldgate, and I met two of the guys that did the

My Consul 1958

piling, and they told me that they were working round the corner with Terry and told me to go and see him.

I went to see him, and he told me to start next morning, so I got my wish to work outside and because it was getting near winter, I had mixed feelings, but it was my chance and I took it. I phoned Jack to tell him, and he was disappointed to lose me and tried to persuade me to go back with him, but I told him that I had got a job already and that was it.

So, I started next morning, the job was hard work and dangerous, especially as I was working with a machine driver who was not particularly good.

My brother John came to London, and he stayed with me in the flat and Terry gave him a job with me; he did not like the cold, but he stayed because he wanted to save some money to go back and buy a taxi. One day I told John I would be driving a machine before long, and he said the governors won't let you, and I said we will see.

As soon as he had enough money, he went back to Malta.

Terry kept me working with him as long as he could. On one job I was on, the machine driver did not come in, so Andy asked me to drive the machine. And with one man not two, we did the same as we had done before for the three days that the machine driver was out. Not long afterwards, I started to meet racism again when another foreman refused to take me to work with them. But because there were no other labourers, they had to use me, but after a few days things got better with every foreman. I think it was a case of making contact. One foreman was getting a crew together and he was looking for labour, and the yard man suggested taking me. The foreman passed some nasty remark, so I walked away to the toilet. He followed me in and asked me if I wanted to go with him. I said, 'I am here to go to work,' so he said, 'Go to the office and get the address.'

After about a year, I was sent to a big job in Paddington, London. There were 18 machines working very close together. One day I could have been hurt badly so I did not go back, not even for my wages, so the foreman Charlie who was racist had a field day telling everybody that I was in prison and other rumours.

While I was out of work, I thought I would do a bit of work on the flat, the floorboards were not very level, so I thought I would phone Jack and ask if he could sell me a couple of bundles of cardboard he used as filling in the handbags, and he told me to go and get them.

By this time, I must have had my first car, a Consul Mark II. I went to pick them up and asked for Jack, and he came to see me. He just said hello and called the foreman and told him, 'Give Charlie what he wants and do not charge for them.' I had a chat with Phil the foreman because Jack could not speak to me.

After a month or so, Terry got in touch with me and told me about the rumours, I told him my version of the story and he told me that he was going to a job in Swansea, South Wales and asked me to go with him and drive a machine, so I said yes and made arrangements for travelling. I met Terry and Bill, the other rig machine driver, and all the way he kept telling me how good he was, and he had been driving for 14 years, but he seemed to be a nice guy and told me he would help me if I needed it.

We started, and I took charge of the machine and one of my labourers told me that he was told he was the driver, but Terry told him that I was the driver, and he and his friend did not like it. But I could handle the men, and they soon learned where they stood.

It was just before Good Friday and Terry was a big fan of West Ham football team, and because we used to work on Good Friday, and West Ham were playing on a Saturday, he suggested that if we worked longer days and did enough work, we could finish on Thursday instead of Saturday, so we tried to do the work to cover us for the two days.

My team did my work and half of the work of the other team, so we left on the Thursday and we were all happy. We got back after a long weekend, and Terry was happy because West Ham won.

One day one of the local foremen visited Terry and when he saw me driving, he asked if the company was making Indians drive now. The job finished, and I was sent to a big job in London with another five men. We were doing a job together and the under foreman told me to go labouring.

I told him that I was a driver and he had other labour to use, he went to tell the foreman, a Charlie – remember him because he was a racist and I will mention him again – so Charlie came and told me to go labouring. I told him I was not going, and he told me to be careful because I was sent to him to sack me. As you know by

Me and Terry on Mumbles Beach, Swansea

now, threats don't worry me, so I told him to do what he likes, and he walked away. In the meantime, Terry phoned and I went with him the next morning.

Of course, I worked with other foremen and two of the foremen I got on with were the two that refused to employ me when I first started.

One of the foremen was quite insulting, and if he thought he could get away with it, he was terrible, but when he tried with me, I stood up to him and he never did it again.

I was sent to work with Charlie again, and every morning Charlie used to collect the buckets, but when he came, I refused to let him have mine, he used to send one of his helpers to pick it up.

One dark night, I asked the inspector to check my pile and the next morning while I was putting on my working clothes, one of the helpers asked me who checked the pile, and I told him who checked it. Next minute, the two helpers came laughing and asked again, and I told them the same story. They went back laughing because they knew what Charlie was up to, the three appeared and Charlie asked the same question, and I told him he could have saved a lot of time if he asked the inspector. With that, he went away with the two helpers laughing behind his back.

We were on piecework and every man for himself, so it was fertile ground for bullying. I did not have a lot of trouble except for a couple of the boys. One was called John, a Londoner, he thought he was the best looker, the best fighter, and the best machine driver, so there was always a bit of friction between us.

We were working in Bethnal Green in London, and we were working next to each other, and he was putting his pile spoil where I was going next, so I told him to stop but he did not. So, in front of him, I went to tell the foreman. He was standing at the edge of a three-metre hole that we were working in. As I was telling the foreman, John stuck two fingers up at me, so I jumped down the hole, ran to John and challenged him to do it again. But he did not. I think when he saw me jump down, he realised that I meant it. A while after we were working in the City of London in the middle of winter, and because I was doing well, the other drivers said that I had the best tools. One morning I had no work to do so I was standing by a fire. John took one of my tools, and before long he was in trouble with it, so I started laughing at him. He ran over to me and said that he would not hesitate to punch me. I said to him it was a bit too early at the moment because it was about eight thirty, we could sort it out at teatime if he wanted and he went away. He started driving and I stayed by the fire. He freed the tool, stopped, and started walking towards me again. As he approached me, he said, 'Charlie, I did not mean anything earlier.'

After that, we became friends, although I used to upset him quite a lot, especially when I used to get lifts from the crane as soon as I needed it and he had to wait. It was only because I used to give the crane driver and the banks man a packet of cigarettes a week and it was worth it.

The other bully was Tommy, an Irishman. He was a rough person and often bullied men. One day in the middle of winter, we were working in Oxford, and one morning, Tommy came to my rig and demanded the dumper from one of my labourers. I walked over to him, and swearing I told him to go and tell his labourer what to do, not my labourer. We used to measure with a steel chain, and he grabbed it and walked away in temper. As he walked by another Irishman, he hit him with the steel chain in the face; it must have hurt in that cold weather. As it happens, the supervisor was on site, so I went and told him that he should sack him but he did not. One day about six of us drivers were sent to do some concrete in a yard for another department, and the supervisor, a Mr Oates, came to talk to us about the job and asked one of the drivers how many drivers among us, and when he said all of us, the supervisor said, 'Do they make foreigners as drivers?' I thought, *My time will come.*

One interesting job I was on was in Guildford, Surrey. We were doing the foundation for the Yvonne Arnaud Theatre. It was on an island in the middle of a river and because it was named after a famous actress, a famous actor, a Michael Redgrave, well known in cinema and theatre, was coming to do the first pile. A lot of preparation had to be done, and the architect got incredibly involved.

Mr Oates wanted to use his machine for publicity, and after calling me a foreigner, I had an argument with him that my machine should be used. The architect heard the argument and told Mr Oates to leave the site and take his machine with him.

The foreman told all his neighbours that he was going to be on telly and his wife was looking forward to seeing him. I discussed with the architect what we were going to do when the film star was going to perform, and everything was agreed. Only the foreman came over and told me that he was going to show the film star what to do because his wife was expecting to see him. But again, the architect came to my rescue and insisted that I do the showing.

The day arrived, and the BBC TV crew arrived at eight am and others followed, there were probably about 30 photographers all waiting for Mr Redgrave to arrive, who was due at 10 am.

Before he arrived, the BBC man asked me to do a bit of driving and he filmed it. He arrived and he looked as if he was ready for the occasion. The architect told him what was to be done with all the cameras clicking. I showed him how to drive the machine but he struggled to make it work, so I had to help him and that was done with, and everything went as the architect planned it. After that, we all looked forward to seeing it on telly at night when we arrived home.

We got home, and the foreman's neighbours were all waiting to see him on the telly, but his wife and the neighbours were all disappointed because Michael did not appear except as one of the crowd, only me the film star and architect appeared, and Michael was seen with the rest of the big crowd that gathered for the occasion. It was only on telly for a few seconds, and they showed Sir Michael driving and the bit of film they took when I was driving, it looked very good. The foreman ended up with his wife telling him that it was not worth watching.

EVENING STANDARD, THURSDAY, OCTOBER 4, 1962—19

SIR MICHAEL SINKS THE FIRST PILE

Sir Michael Redgrave, in a white overall borrowed from a workman, pulls the lever to drive the first pile for the foundations of a new theatre, today.

Work on the new Yvonne Arnaud Theatre, at Guildford, Surrey, started officially this morning.

Sir Michael is to direct the theatre's opening festival in the summer of 1964.

Yvonne Arnaud Theatre Guildford with Sir Michael
Redgrave driving the first pile 1963

A few days later the architect gave me a few photos
and suggested I go to the High Street and see all the
photos in the windows, so the next day at dinner time I
had a walk to see for myself all the windows of the
shops. I was pleased to see that the windows had a lot
of photos showing Sir Michael and me and the architect.

A few days later I went to Oxford Street to take a
photo for my passport, and two young women were
going to take the photos. They looked at me and asked
me if I was in show business or a wrestler because they
had seen me before and, of course, I said I was not a

public person. A few days after I was thinking about the two girls in the photo shop, and a thought went to my mind if they had seen my photos in the shops in Guildford!

I went to work one Saturday to a job in Mortlake, South London, next to the River Thames. We went in to finish the job because it had to finish that week. As it happens, it was a bad day, my machine broke down and another machine that I started using also broke down. Luckily there was another machine I could use. After a while, people started coming to the riverbanks and as the crowd got bigger, I asked Terry what was happening. He said it was the boat race that happens every year, and it started about 4pm, and we would be able to watch it because it finished where we were. It was interesting because I had never heard of it before.

Every job we started, the manager in charge of the job used to set a bonus target and, of course, he used to try to save some money. Sometimes we haggled for days and I used to end up as spokesman and I enjoyed it. The governors liked to talk to me because I used to talk sense, and they never seemed to hold it against me, and never made any racial remarks. To save me from boring you, I will just mention two jobs which might be of interest. When negotiations got difficult, the supervisor got involved; he was a Mr George Kemp who came from the north of England. He was a hard man, he knew his job, and he was also a fair man; of course he had his faults the same as everybody else.

We were doing the foundations for Wembley Park Station and the job was not going very well, and we were arguing about the bonus. After a few days, Mr Kemp and the engineer in charge of the job and a director came to sort it out after Mr Kemp had a good look round because he used to do that all the time. He went in the office where the other two were and they called me in to have a sensible word with me to sort things out. After a small discussion, I told them that the site mixer was not fast enough, but they explained that the main contractor was in charge and they could not do anything about it.

As I was supposed to be talking to the brains of the company, I thought I would be a bit sarcastic, and I said, 'If you look out of the window and see a ready-mix concreter going by and ask him to come in the gate, he will fill the pile in no time at all.' They looked at each other, and Mr Kemp said, 'Charlie is right,' and said they will investigate it, and that was the first time we used ready-mix concrete. Another job I like to talk about was on the Isle of Sheppey in Kent. It was a big job for Abbot's Laboratories – they are in the news about the virus we have now. There were 18 rigs, the highest number of rigs I had ever been on. We started on one part of the site and as the job progressed, most of the rigs were moved to a different part of the site, and

I was left to finish where I was. The men on the other side were not happy with the bonus, so we went on strike and the foreman phoned the office and he was told that they were getting the right money, so we went to work. Later that day, I saw all the local labour sitting on a heap of clay, so I went to ask what was happening, and they told me that the local labour were not getting the rise. With that, I had a go at the drivers and told them the labourers stuck with them in the morning and they should stick with them now because on their own, they had no chance. So they agreed, went back to work, and I told the foreman that unless somebody from the office came to see us in the morning, we were going on strike.

Abbott Laboratories, Isle of Sheppey. Checking a pile

Next morning, Mr Kemp arrived, and we went to see him. We started the discussions and one of the guys said something out of place, and Mr Kemp told him to piss off, and with that we all walked out. It was a Thursday, and we used to get paid on Thursday, so we had to wait for the wages. Some of the boys went to a pub. I went up the road and got another job.

When I got back, I decided to wash my car, and Mr Kemp came over and said, 'You're alright, why are you not working? You are getting all the money you agreed.' So I said, 'I earn my living with you, and I work with the men.' He asked me if I could get a couple of sensible men so we could have a chat. So I went to the pub and picked three and asked if the other men would be happy with what we agreed, and they accepted, so we went to see Mr Kemp. I think everybody wanted to go back to work, so because I was happy with my deal, I was sort of independent, I did all the talking and everything was sorted.

On the Isle of Sheppey there were a lot of holiday camps, and we used to go there for a drink every night, good music and plenty of drinks because after all the negotiation, we were earning good money. All the young men on site were local, and although I used to go out some nights with one of them, most nights I used to go with men a lot older than me. We used to be having a quiet drink when one of them would go and get a tray full of whiskey, and they used to drink a lot.

One night, whilst driving home, one of the guys in the back of the car had his elbow in my back and was provoking me and trying to cause me to crash because he wanted to see what it was like to be in a car crash.

CHAPTER 21

MY FRIENDS

One of the men was Jim. He was a lot older than me but for some reason he sort of adopted me and we became very friendly. Jim was a very good piano player and he was very good at singing old cockney songs; some of them were dirty.

He used to play the piano in a pub in East London, but back to holiday camps. When the band had a break, sometimes the guys used to get on the stage and do the entertainment. Jim was on the piano, the foreman played the spoons, one was a good singer, and one thought he could act but he was embarrassing, but the holidaymakers used to like them.

I used to give them a lift home when we came home for the weekend, and sometimes Jim asked me to go to his home and have a cup of coffee. I met his wife who was a lot younger than Jim, and right away she told me that things were not very good between her and Jim. She was very open from the first day, they had a teenage daughter and they always made me very welcome. They must have thought a lot of me because one day the wife asked me if I came from a well to do family in Malta.

I used to go and have a drink with Jim some weekends and hear him playing the piano. I normally went to clubs up the West End but I liked the old East End pubs with an old piano in the corner and the cockney songs. The pubs I used to go to was when there was a talent show and the singers were special, none of the karaoke of today.

Two friends I had, one was Peter and the other was Lino, were both good dancers. I don't remember how I got involved with them, but I was never short of friends.

Lino came from Rabat in Malta and was the best Maltese ballroom dancer in England, and Peter was the best rock n roll Maltese dancer in England, and I used to go to the dance hall with one or the other, and I could not put two feet together. I think I went to all the dance halls in London, but I used to love to see the dancing. I will come to Peter later.

One night I went with Lino and his girlfriend, a Maltese girl, to a club in Soho, West London, that I used to go to frequently. We got a drink and I lit one of my King Edward cigars, putting it in a big cigar holder I had. As I lit it, Lofty's girlfriend came over and asked for a couple of puffs like she always did whenever I lit a cigar. Lofty was a very big man, hence the nickname, never passed any comment but I did know how he felt about it.

The night came to an end, and on the way out, Lofty pinched Lino's girlfriend's bum and she created a scene. So Lino started to have a go at Lofty. Lino was in front, the girl behind him, and I was at the back. Things got a bit hot, and Lofty made a charge for Lino as I happened to be going through a door, so I put my hand across the door and stopped Lofty and told him to stop. Luckily, he stopped and I managed to cool them down so much they got in the road outside hugging and kissing each other and me wondering what I could have got myself into.

By the way, Lino was justified to have a fight over his girlfriend because a few days later she finished with him, and a few nights later she was in my bed, at her instigation, of course, because I thought she was trouble. Back to Peter. He was into everything, besides being a good dancer, he was involved in some crime.

We used to go to all the dance halls in London, and once they made a rock n roll film and Peter was in it. He had a partner but he always had his own dancing partner. We used to dance in a hall in Mile End and it was full of Maltese guys, and that's where Peter and Lino used to meet and start showing off. Lino did not like to see me with Peter and he stopped going out with me.

Besides going to dance halls, we use go to the West End clubs and sometimes I used to take two weeks off work and spend the nights in clubs, come out at six in the morning and he used to dance all night. Sometimes we used to go on our own and we used to visit different clubs. One night we were invited to go to a private strip show because at that time they were not licensed. It was in a room upstairs in Old Compton Street, and after that we went to a few of them, one was in Leicester Square in a basement.

Peter was a hustler. He used to come to my flat and as soon as I opened the door, he would ask me if I had something to eat because he was starving. One time I said I had some bread, and it was a bit dry, and he said kick it all over the floor and I will eat it.

Other times as I opened the door, he'd say, 'Get dressed. We are going out,' and show me a big bundle of notes. We used to go to a Maltese club in Islington and play poker; sometimes he played and sometimes I played as partners sharing the money. One night he was playing, and he was doing well. After a while, one game got a bit serious with a lot of money involved and one of the players increased the bet with a big sum, so Peter lost his nerve and asked me what I thought. The guy that put the bet on the table with all the money in the air asked how many men he was playing against. And you can imagine the commotion that happened after that, and that was the last time we played poker. As I said, Peter was involved in some crime, and one morning at five there was knock on my front door. I opened the door and two police officers asked me if they could come in, so I let them in. They had a look round the flat, and in the lounge I had a drinking bar, and at the back wall I had a shotgun and a guitar hanging in a cross fashion, so right away they thought they'd got me. They asked what I was doing with a shotgun. I told them that I had a permit to go and shoot game on a farm, so I showed them the permit and they left. Peter had a brother and he came to see me and told me that Peter was arrested the same morning. He went to see him and took him a cake because it was his birthday but the warden told him he would only get the cake if he told him all about me. The warden wanted to know what I did for a living and all sorts of questions.

Having a drink after work in a holiday camp
on the Isle of Sheppey

After that, I think I was watched all the time. I was working on a job in the West End of London, it was between two roads, and as I went in one gate I saw a squad car in front of the other gate looking in. Later that morning, the police came to see the foreman. I asked the foreman if the police asked him about me and he said no, but he did not tell me what they came to see him about.

Another day I had a day off work and went to a street market in Shoreditch and bought some vegetables and some other things and put them all on the back seat and covered them, and I went to a café in Islington to see a friend called Philipp. As I stopped in front of the café, two police in normal clothes got out of a van and came towards me from both sides of the car and asked me to open the boot to have a look at what's inside. I opened the boot and there was nothing in it. They never wanted to see what was under the blanket on the back seat because they saw me put the stuff in there, so they must have been following me all morning, but asked me to put my belongings in the boot. By this time, a lot of people had gathered round, and they asked me to empty my pockets and put it on the boot. I asked why and they said here or the station so I chose to go to the station. One of them came in the car with me and the other drove the van.

I was taken in a room and asked to put my things on the table, so I did and there was nothing illegal. One of them left the room and returned with another officer.

He took the investigation over and asked me to take my shoes off. I got really worried because I knew what they were looking for, drugs. I took my shoes off and again there was nothing, then he put his hands in my pockets and found nothing and told the others to search the car again. I sat on a chair to put my shoes on and asked what is this because I work for a living. He rushed over to me with his face close to my face and started insulting me, hoping that I would retaliate but I kept cool because I realised he wanted a result. As we were walking back to the car, one of them told me never to volunteer to go to the station, but again, they did not find anything. Another day I was out with a friend of mine called Freddie and we had been to a shop that mended my shoes which had rubber soles. As I parked across the road from my flat, a squad car pulled up behind me; as we got out of the car a policeman who must have been waiting for me a few doors from my door started walking towards me, and one from the squad car so we met outside my door.

One asked me what was in the bag, and I told him it was a pair of shoes that I just picked from the menders. So he had a look and said I did not know you could mend this, and all cocky I said, 'You know now.' With that, they went away and me and Fred went in, Fred first. As I closed the door behind me, I slumped back against it and Fred asked me what the matter was, so

I got some dope out of my pocket and showed him and he asked what it was; I realised what a narrow escape I had.

Another day I arrived with some of my friends at my flat and parked across the road, and opened the front door so my friends could go in, and I started taking some stolen car radios.

As I picked some and started walking across the road to my flat, a guy standing by my car shouted hello. I looked back and told him I would be back in a minute. I started to think, *Is he tall enough to be a policeman?* and all sorts of things went through my mind. I told my friends to stay in whatever happens so I went out to face the music. As I approached him, he said, 'I think you have a puncture.' I nearly said I could kiss you, but I said thank you and he went away. That was the longest few minutes I went through in my life.

Peter came out of prison and opened a café in Dalston, East London, and he was doing well. Fred and me were going to take it over. We agreed to try it for a week and we started on a Monday morning. Late morning, this crowd of men, about six of them, came in and ordered coffee and sat down. Peter introduced them and one was Jim, a big man, and he seemed to be the leader of the gang, and he seem to be a decent guy and was friendly with Peter. A while later about six men arrived, and they did not seem to be very friendly, they barely talked to anybody; they stayed for a while and went. After Jim and his gang went as well and after lunch, we were not busy, so we asked Peter about the gangs. Peter told us that Jim and his gang were ok, but the other gang had a very bad name. They used to ask for protection money from shops and the stalls in the market but they left Peter alone because Jim looked after him.

Peter thought that the other gang kidnapped girls and they were never seen again, and one of the girls was a friend of one of Jim's boys but they did not have proof of it, so they were not friends. After hearing all that, Sam and I started to think about getting involved with the café, but we thought we would wait a day or two before we said anything.

About 10 in the morning the next day, the bad gang came in, and when they saw Jim's gang was not around, they tried to show their authority. One of them went behind the counter and kissed Peter's girlfriend. Freddy happened to be behind the counter as well and punched him as quick as blinking an eye. They left right away and said they would be back to make sure that Fred won't be able to do that again.

Jim and his gang arrived because they were always together and Peter told them all what happened. Jim said, we are here because we have been trying to pick a fight with them because of the girl they thought they kidnapped. We thought we would get ready for them as well, and I had a handgun and Joe had a small-bore shotgun and a handgun as well.

We got the guns behind the counter ready for any occasion that might happen, and Jim and his gang stayed in all the time. It started getting late, after dark, and we started to wonder if they were coming. About 11pm about 10 cars arrived and parked near the café and the gang started coming into the café but when they saw Jim and his gang most of the other guys got in their cars and went away. The bad boys came in all holding big screwdrivers and shifting spanners and a big knife, enormously proud of themselves, showing off and swinging the weapons around a dog we had. The tension was beginning to mount, and Jim told us Maltese and Peter's girlfriend to go behind the counter. He leaned back against the counter and opened the long coat he used to wear and a big belt with a big buckle he used to wear, the leader asked Jim if he joined the war, and Jim said, 'It's up to you what I do,' and with that, the gang left.

A few nights after, as I dropped Jim and his gang outside the café, a squad car pulled up in front of me. One policeman came out of the back seat and as he was walking towards me, shouted the engine's still running. He told me to switch the engine off and to get out of the car. I don't remember what happened after that because, as you know, I was used to that sort of thing. One night, Peter and I went for a drink and ended up having a drink with three guys that had just come out of prison for killing a gangster in West London. It wasn't long before the conversation got on to Malta having problems with independence from England, and one said we got to do something here, and the best he could think of was to put a bomb in the Underground and blow a hole under the Thames.

When you hear these words in a drinking place, right away you think the beer is talking, but these guys had just come out of prison for killing a gangster in cold blood and for some technical thing, they got away with a light sentence. I got worried because I did not want to get involved with anything like that, and because I learned the character of these guys, I started thinking how I was going to get out of it because if I told them I didn't want to be involved, they would tell me, 'You have to be involved because you know and we don't trust you.'

The evening finished and me and Peter left. I asked Peter how we were going to get out of the situation and he said "they will forget about it, thank God", it was the beer talking.

I had a friend who lived in a cul-de-sac in Whitechapel in East London, and I used to visit him very often, and I made friends with Joe and Steve, who was married, and both came from Sliema. Joe was single, he was older than me, but we got on well together, and we used to go out to clubs.

One Saturday, Freddy and me went to pick Joe up and he had a friend with him, and Joe asked me if his

Turkey

friend could come with us, so I said yes. As soon as we got in the club, the friend got into a conversation with a cross dresser that I knew well and he told me that the guy tried to chat him up. I said to him to let him have a feel to see what happens.

By this time, he was getting on our nerves, and after a while we went to a club that was owned by Joe's friend. It was up a long flight of stairs, so we had a drink and ordered a steak and chips and we sat at the counter. The guy sat in the corner and Fred and me each side of him, so when I talked to him, Fred pinched some chips and when Fred talked to him, I pinched the chips; he did not like it and tried to stab us with the fork. Eventually we got a chair, and the guy got a bit rowdy, so the club owner asked Joe if this guy was a friend of his and to my surprise Joe said no. The club owner made a gesture with his head and the chucker-out went behind the guy, lifted him up and threw him down the stairs. When we were going down, he was still down the bottom moaning with pain, so I said to Joe to take him home, and Joe said to leave him there. I asked the guy if he had any money and he said no, so I gave him some money and got him to a taxi and sent him home and that was the last I saw of him.

Joe got me a garage near their garage, and it was full of junk. I cleared it all up, and I still have some screws that I found.

When driving, I was a bit mad. One night I was coming from Southend and the car in front would not move over, so I overtook it on the inside and pulled in front of it and touched the front of it. They took my number and reported me and although the police did not find any marks on my car, they still took me to court in Brentwood, Essex. Somebody recommended this city lawyer that I used and as soon as the judge sat down, he approached the bench and asked if the judge could see to us first and the judge told him to sit down and wait his turn. My case came up and the judge looked at us, and without any questions, he fined me

£90 and a year's licence. I went back to the garage and jacked the car up on bricks and waited.

After six months, I applied for the licence, but I was refused. I started thinking about the day I would start the car again, and because Joe and Steve used to spray cars at the weekends, I asked if they'd spray my car. But when I told them how I wanted my car sprayed, they told me that I must mark the design myself because they did not want to be responsible for doing it wrong.

I brought something from Malta to go on the bonnet and we were ready to start. They did a good job and every time I stopped, everyone used to look at it, including the police. As one of them put it, 'your car sticks out like a sore thumb' when he stopped me in West London. The police started to give me a lot of attention again and they used to stop me at every chance they found, it was so bad that I went to see a lawyer about it, but he told me that he could not do anything.

Fred was another friend I had, and we bought a house to let. He lived in one room and we used to let the other rooms, and I used to do the letting and collect rent. At one time, we had two young women living in one room, and every time I went to collect the rent, they used to ask me if they could pay in kind, but I refused the opportunity because I wanted to collect the rent. One night, Fred, me, Sam, and one other went to a club up the West End, and well into the night when we had a few drinks, I was sitting at a table, and Sam came over and told me that he was going to hit this other Maltese guy and I did not try to stop him. I went in the toilets to freshen up and sat down again and as Sam hit the Maltese guy, about 20 English boys started on my friends, so I went to help. Before I even started, I got glassed in my forehead so I could not see a thing with the blood that was coming out of my head.

A boy and two girls guided me up the stairs and I went to sit in the car to wait for my friends. A policeman asked me what I was doing and when he saw my face, he escorted me to a police station. He asked me what happened, and I asked him for a mirror, and he said, laughing, 'Your face does not look very pretty right now,' and told me to get going.

I looked for my friends but they were nowhere to be seen. On the way home, I caught up with them and they got in the car and we went to my flat, licking our wounds.

The next night, two of my friends went back to the club and someone told them that one of the guys that fought us had a big cut in his arm and had to have some stitches.

If you lived in the Brick Lane area, you get involved with some shady people. Sometimes I used to eat in Indian cafes and sometimes in Maltese cafes. Once, I was eating my dinner and this big guy called the mule that I knew came in and sat on my table and started talking to me normally. A few minutes later, two policemen came in, grabbed him and took him away; I heard afterwards that he killed an Indian with a brick.

An ice cream I had in Corfu
13 Euros each

One night I was home, and I decided to go to a pub a few metres from my flat for a quiet drink. I ordered a drink, and as soon as I sat by a table, a man of about 40, a man my age and a woman my age came in, and the old man asked me if they could sit at my table although there were empty tables. I said yes and they sat down. He and the girl seemed to be very friendly and I started wondering about the relationship between them, then the old man said I am Joe the pin and I realised who he was. He was a Gozo man, well known for using the knife as soon as looking at you. The girl was his daughter and the man was just a friend.

Joe asked me where I lived and when I told him, the girl volunteered to come and have a cup of coffee when we finished, so we went to the flat and on the way I started wondering what I was getting involved in. My kitchen was in a separate room. I told them to make themselves at home and I went to make the coffee. The girl said, 'I will come to give you a hand,' and my worries increased. As soon as we got in the kitchen, she said, 'I can only give you a kiss because I am flying the red flag.' Right away, I started breathing a bit better, so we had the coffee and they left, and I waved them goodbye and good riddance.

I started going out with a girl called Sheila, and one afternoon I had to go to Romford, Essex, to do an errand. I did the errand and I was returning to my flat when a taxi pulled in front of me at Mile End and blocked me. Two guys came out and one started shouting, 'Next time you go up West End, you are going to get slaughtered.' So I started to weigh the situation up. I looked at the taxi driver and he winked at me for reassurance.

I noticed the one behind had something in his shirt because there was a big lump, but the first man said something was going to happen in the future, and because the driver winked at me, I thought they were not going to do anything today, so I was relieved. I asked what the problem was and he said that girl was his girlfriend and he wanted her back. I said it is up to the girl what she does. If she doesn't want to come with you she won't. And Steve said I only want to talk to her, so I asked her, and she agreed to go with them, and I agreed to meet him at Whitechapel in one hour. As I was driving towards my flat to get my gun, you can imagine what state of mind I was in. I stopped at the lights and a car ran into the back of my car at high speed. You can imagine the shock I got into, I just did not know what happened and if the guys had done it. I got out of the car and there was a drunken man standing there and he said, 'I am sorry.' The police arrived and the man was nowhere to be seen, so the police told me to go to the nearest police station to make a statement. In the meantime, Steve and Sheila arrived and said that she had chosen to stay with me. Steve said to me, 'She's got my ring and I want it back.' So we agreed that he would come with me to the Police Station and go afterwards to get the ring. As we were going, Steve asked where I worked and when I told him, he said, 'My brother-in-law works for them; his name is Joe and he is a lorry driver,' and I said, 'I know him.'

We got to the police station. I made a statement, and we went back to the flat and I gave him the ring and took him home.

Joe was a nice man, and I told him that I met his brother-in-law Steve and he made it clear that Steve was no good. A few days later, Steve knocked on my door, and as soon as I let him in, he started telling me how desperate he was for money and I knew what was coming. Steve started playing with his hands, and on one I could see a penknife taped to it, and after a while, he told me how good it is to slash somebody in the face. I started looking around the room for protection, near one of the armchairs, I noticed a walking stick a friend forgot to take home, so I sat on it. Steve asked me for some money, and I said I barely have money for myself, so Steve got down on his knees to beg me again and I told him I got no money. With that, he started to argue with me, telling me he did not like to be refused.

Now I thought it was time to tell him to go, so he got up and went and I followed him to the car, and the driver was waiting for him. I said to Steve not to come again. The driver said, 'You want to be careful, you live on the ground floor and we can throw a firebomb through the window and burn you out.' My answer was, 'You might start a war, but I will finish it,' and they left.

I always knew some shady men, and one of them was Jack, a Scotsman with a very bad reputation, so I thought I would go and have a word with him. I told him the situation with Steve, and I pretended to be afraid of what they might do because I had to be careful that Jack was not a friend of Steve's and I would be the victim. Jack told me to go and see him in a couple of days to see who this Steve was because it is not the man you've got to worry about but who was backing him. He could be one of a big gang and they'd be after you.

A few days after, I went to see Jack, and he told me he found out that Steve was nothing and if I wanted, he would sort him out. I did not want to make it obvious and again I played the scared theme, so he said leave it with me; I will sort it out.

A week later, I saw Joe, and he said did you hear about my brother-in-law Steve? Some bloke gave him a good hiding and he threw his bike in the Thames. I asked him if Steve said who the bloke was, and Joe said Steve had no idea. I went to see Jack, took a couple of bottles of drinks to thank him and we had a drink and I left. I never heard of Steve again and hoped that it was the last time I got involved with bad boys.

CHAPTER 22

I BUY MY FIRST HOUSE

I carried on with my work and enjoyed it, and one day I was sent to a job in Poole in Dorset, a beautiful county. The foreman was Harry, one of the foremen that refused to use me because I was a foreigner, but we were OK by now. On a Monday, I picked up Harry and two labourers and travelled in my car to Poole, it took us five hours because there were no motorways those days. We found some lodgings and went to have a look at the job. It was on the shore at the edge of the sea, and Dorset was a beautiful county and it looked all good. Our lodgings were good, a nice landlady, and the food seemed to be very good. The next morning we started, and the job was going very well, we used to come home at the weekend in my car.

One weekend, I was supposed to pick up Harry at four in the morning but I overslept. I had no phone so I could not phone Harry to tell him I would be late, so I rushed to Dagenham and I got to where Harry lived but he had already left the house. I caught up with him as he was turning round the corner. I called him, and he heard me and came to the car, and I wished he didn't because he started moaning because I was late. He said if we got to the job late, he would sack me, so I got fed up and I told him to hold on to the dashboard and shut up till we get to the job, and if I was late he could do what he liked.

I thought I would see how long it took Harry to lose his bottle because I was going to try to get to Poole in less than five hours.

So I opened up and started racing from the start, and I went to pick the two labourers, and when I say racing, I meant it by going on the right of the Keep Left signs, and I did that a few times. By the time we got out of London, Harry never took his hands off the dashboard and never said a word till we got halfway when he asked me to stop in a service station because he needed to go to the toilets. I responded by saying we will be late, and I carried on and got to the job at seven thirty, and I said you can buy me breakfast, and we made it to the nearest café. I enjoyed the job and the area, and me and Harry used to go out at night sometimes to Bournemouth and sometimes to country pubs in the area where we knew we could find some local girls.

One night we took two girls home and I dropped Harry and his girlfriend, and I went to take my girlfriend home and agreed to pick up Harry later, of course, as we were in a strange place.

I had not been there before, so when I dropped my girl, I had to go and find Harry in the dark. I had driven into a dead-end lane and as I was reversing, my front wheel dropped in some hole. I got a torch from the boot of the car and I saw the wheel in a ditch, so I decided to put the car in reverse and hope for the best. By this time, I had no idea where I had dropped Harry but I kept looking until I managed to drive near him and he shouted for me to stop. He got in the car and started threatening me with the sack, so I said I might as well drop you here if you are going to sack me in the morning. With that he stopped. As it happened, the foremen at that time all they did was use the sack as their weapon.

When we finished the job and were coming home, and as I said before there were no motorways, as I was overtaking and somehow the car lost power and I was stuck in the middle of the road. I could not pull in with a car coming fast towards me, it was a bit scary, which is why I still remember it today. Somehow, I managed to get in and we were safe. I stopped the car and found one of the spark plugs wire was loose.

When I drove a few miles further, there were two bodies of motorbike riders' dead on the verge with their faces covered with a blanket, but I could see their boots. After my narrow escape, I felt my legs going very weak and I slowed down till I got better. A few weeks after that I bought my first house, a Victorian four-storey house and what a state it was in, top to bottom.

One day we were taking the wallpaper off and I realised there were a lot of layers, I counted nine layers; that was in one of the rooms in the basement.

I was a bit lucky because about seven or eight of my friends used to come and give me a hand on a Sunday, and to get the best out of them, I used to put them in different rooms to stop them from talking too much.

One day, in one of the top rooms, the ceiling was dropping down and we were discussing when we were going to do it, and one of them started on it and before you know it, it was finished; that's how helpful they were. We always used to have a good laugh about one thing or another.

When they arrived in the morning, I used to prepare a big breakfast to start them in the right mood, and for lunch I used to do a nice roast and they looked forward to it, and after a big meal, they would go home happy. A couple of months after I bought the house, I was offered a foreman job and it was in Hatch End in North London. It was a fair-sized job and I came across Charlie, the racist guy, but now he was a supervisor. One day he brought some papers to fill in but I was getting some milk when he came.

He just left the papers and left, and when I got back the boys told me that Charlie came and left right away, so I thought he would report me that I was not on the job. So I went on the phone to George Kemp, the head supervisor, and as an excuse I told him what happened and asked how to fill the forms in because Charlie did not show me. He told me that Charlie had been on and told him that he waited for me a long time, so I told him how long I was and he said I will have a word with him, and that was the beginning of a new confrontation with Charlie.

Next, I was doing a job at West Drayton near Heathrow, and as it happens, the other two supervisors were on site when Charlie arrived, so he tried to catch me out, but his brain was slower than mine and he made a fool of himself in front of the other two, who by this time were laughing at him. The site manager was a younger person, a bit of a bighead, but I got on well with him until one morning he sacked the only man working for him who was also a friend of his for nothing.

The job was getting near completion and the contractor started excavating my work, and the manager called me in the office and told me that one of my piles was out of position. He started to show his personality by trying to intimidate and bully me. I told him that I had already had a look at the work and found nothing wrong with it. He told me that he would phone the office and ask them what they were going to do about it, so I told him again that the work was done within the tolerances. When he persisted, I got some money out of my pocket and said I would pay for the phone call because a few weeks ago I was driving one of them machines and I liked it, and what's the worst that could happen, and I am waiting for you to make the phone call.

He paused for a minute or two and looked at me as if to say you win and said I will let it go this time and the job was finished. Back to my first house. It was a four-storey Victorian house with a semi-basement in a nice road in Forest Gate, East London, but in an awfully bad state and had to be refurbished top to bottom. My intention was to turn it into four flats, so I started working after work and weekends and got some tradesmen to do the gas and electric works. With 10 rooms to refurbish, it was a big task to do and I wondered where to start the work and would I ever finish it. I started by clearing all the rubbish and started getting visits from my friends and promises of help.

My friends kept their word and about eight or nine promised to come on a Sunday and help, so I made sure that I had enough food for them and if they thought that they were coming to meet all the friends and have a laugh and go home I had work in mind. I got up early and prepared two big dishes of meat, potatoes and onions, ready to cook on time.

About 8am, the first arrived and I put him to work, and within half hour about eight arrived, so to stop them talking I put them in separate rooms. When it was possible, they all went to work, and I started the cooking and kept giving the boys advice and help when needed. One or two were painting ceilings and most of them were stripping wallpaper.

Lunch time arrived and we sat down to eat and catch up on the gossip of the previous night. By the time we finished, it was time for them to go home, and as I still lived in my flat, I gave some of them a lift home and they all promised to come next Sunday.

A few days after, I met a Maltese family. Paul, Mary, and a few kids. Mary was the sister of Victor the Teddy boy, you remember him. Paul was involved with a Maltese football team and that's all he used to talk about and kept asking me to go and watch them play, but I was too busy doing the house. My friends were extremely helpful and worked very hard. We were in a room at the top of the house, and we were saying the ceiling got to be replaced and one asked me if I had the plasterboards and when I said yes, he started taking the ceiling down and in a little while three of us had the plaster boards put up and the job was done; that's how helpful they were.

While all that was happening, I met Pat, who was to become my future wife, and we started living in the flat until I finished the basement flat. The house refurbishing was getting finished. I started letting the flats out and before long all the house was full. I finished the basement and Pat and I moved in. After a while, we got our first dog, an Alsatian, and when we got it as a puppy all you could see was his legs, so I named it Bony. He grew up to be a lovely dog, except it hated the postman and every letterbox I made, it destroyed.

After a while, a little girl that lived upstairs was stroking it on the back near his tail, his head turned very quick and I thought it was going to bite the little girl, so I gave it to a guy in a building yard. After that, our first girl Julia was born, a very good girl, never cried at night. If she woke up and started crying, as soon as Pat and I talked to her, she went back to sleep. Paul persuaded me to go and watch his Maltese team, and after I went a few times, Paul for some reason I do not know, asked me to be the team's manager and I accepted, and the team was doing very well.

One evening, myself and three other players went looking for one of the players in Maltese cafes round Aldgate and the police stopped us and told me and the others to get out of the car. One of the men with me had his leg in plaster but he had to get out as well. The police asked me what I was doing going round Maltese cafes. I said we were looking for one of the players, they told me they were going to search the car so I opened the boot and there was nothing in it. They started looking in the car, and under my seat they found a big chopper; they looked at each other and started swinging it around as if to show the people that gathered around that this is what the Maltese get up to. One said to me,

'Are you going to chop this man up when you find him?' and I pointed at the man with the plastered leg and said, 'He is going to do the chopping.' I said I got that chopper because I just cleared a flat that a friend of mine's mother had died in, and I forgot that I put the chopper under the seat after I had chopped most of the furniture. After a few more questions, they told me to be on my way. I stayed for two seasons and I packed it in because I had other things to do.

The kitchen in the basement used to flood when we had heavy rain because the drains could not cope, so I decided to do some improvements in the kitchen area and put a new kitchen and toilet and shower in. So I asked if I could get an anti-flood valve that I could use and I found one in Scotland that cost a packet. I ordered one and the kitchen furniture and started digging the manholes at the back of the house to find the existing drains.

The reason for the manholes was one to connect the anti-flood valve and the other to connect to the main drain. The manholes were over two metres deep. While I was digging, I told my next-door neighbour what I was doing, and he said it was a good idea. The valve arrived, and I concreted it in, ready to be connected.

The furniture for the kitchen arrived and a day after there was a knock on the door and the man said he was a health officer and understood that I was doing some work and he wanted to have a look. So I showed him around and he was very impressed and let it slip that the neighbour phoned the council to see what I was doing to save his house from flooding. The inspector told me I was doing a good job, but I had got to go the right way about it to get a proper drawing made, so I got an architect and he did the drawing, and when I paid him he told me that it was waste of time submitting them because the council would not pass them and to have a word with the district surveyor. He came around and he said no way that I could do the work. I phoned the health inspector and when I told him, he said he'd be there right away. When he came, I told him what happened, and he said he would talk to the district surveyor and he would phone me back in a couple of days. So I waited, and after two days he phoned me and told me how sorry he was, and there was nothing he could do and wished that he had never got involved.

It was heartbreaking when I was filling the manholes with the anti-flood valve concreted in after all that hard work and effort, but I could do nothing about it.

I started looking for another house to live in, and after looking at a few houses, we picked one in Monega Road a couple of streets away from my house and moved in, and our second girl Lisa was born. She was not a happy baby, always crying. We took her to Great Ormond Street to see if there was anything wrong with her, but they found nothing wrong. She was a real rebel, would eat everything and keep crying, making a mess with the food; this created a not very good relationship with her mother.

Because by now I was a staff member of Cementation and on the pension scheme and my family would be looked after, I decided to go to Malta to sort things out. Because all the trouble my mother had because of my uncle dying in New York, I did not want Pat and all the family to have all those problems again, so I made a will that said everything I own in Malta stays in Malta. I was criticised for it by one of my family in later years, but because of the way things turned out, I think it was one of the best decisions I ever made.

The house had an outside toilet and a tin bath in the kitchen, and it was time for me to go to work and put a bathroom and toilet upstairs. I was telling one of the neighbours that I would have a bathroom upstairs in three months and he said it was impossible. I started, and before long I had the job done, and when my neighbour heard the flushing go, they never spoke to us again.

I carried on as a foreman, but when there was no work as a foreman, I went back to driving a machine. One morning I got a message from the office and the manager told me that after the job I did in Hatch End, I left a pile out, and as it was not like me to do that, I should go next morning to see about it. When I got home, I looked for some drawings that I kept as it was my first job, and I found them under the stairs, all bitten

Il-Gimgha, 3 ta' Awissu, 1962.

DIŻI JŻURU LIL
ART TWELIDHOM

Arriving in Malta after nine years in England

by mice. Next morning, I went to meet the site manager and I was not very welcome. Right away he said to me, 'Your company is all problems,' because there was a problem on the previous block but as it happens, it was their problem.

So I asked him to show me which pile was missing, and when we got to the spot and showed me, it was one of a pair right across the line. I opened my drawing and it showed the pair on an angle, so I showed him where the pile was and to get somebody to look for it, and when they dug down, the pile was there. I asked him to take his insults back and he could not apologise enough. I was sent to a job in Falconwood, South London. It was an awkward job because it was on a railway bank that slipped, and we were doing the piling to stabilise it. My job manager was a Mr Michael Adams, who I met for the first time when he came to the site and explained all about the job, and it happens that the people managing the job used to work with Mike in a previous company.

The site manager thought he knew it all, and we started to mark where the first pile had to go. He had no idea and he would not accept that he was wrong, but eventually he gave up and the job was going very well. We came to the end, and Mr Adams and the contract manager met on site, and because the job went so well, the contract manager tried to find something wrong so he could ask for some money back but Mr Adams did not give up. We cleared the site and after a few days,

I got a letter from Mr Adams telling me what a good job I did and he was looking forward to working with me in the future. I bet he never envisaged how long.

I thought I would make some improvements in the house by taking down the chimney breast in the back room and upstairs room, so I changed the car for a van to be able to cart all the rubble away. I wanted to finish before the next baby arrived, but Pat had other ideas and had the twins while I was in the middle of things. I was also working away in Kings Lynne, Norfolk, so I had to come home to be with Pat and finish the rooms. You can imagine what state I was in, looking after the girls, working on the chimneys, and going to see the rest of the family. When the twins were born, Pat said to me, 'You can't recognise which is which.' I told her Joe's ears stuck out.

Lisa carried on eating her favourite dish – soap – so one morning I caught her eating some soap and told her to keep eating, it's alright, and when she stopped, I told her to keep eating. When she started crying, I asked her if she was going to stop eating the soap for good or to keep eating it, so she stopped, and I could carry on with my work.

Among all that confusion, I decided to get a new car to get Pat and the twins from hospital because I only had the van.

I managed to finish the chimney breast and tidy up and got the family home, and thank God all the children

Monument for the fifteenth of August 1942 convoy
that we called the Convoy of Santa Maria

were healthy. The woman neighbour, not the jealous
one, used to help Pat with the babies and we settled to
be a nice family.

We call it the Convoy of Santa Maria because the
convoy that arrived in Malta, which brought an end to
the food and fuel shortages, arrived on 15th August
which is the feast of Our Lady. This is the largest feast
that is celebrated by the Maltese people.

CHAPTER 23

CHANGING MY JOB

Now it was time to go to work again. I was sent to a job in Central Hill, Crystal Palace in South London. It was a big job, but my job was independent from the big job, it was six piles only. The day I finished, the father of the foreman in charge of the big job died, so he had to have a few days off, so I was asked to help the foreman who was second in command.

When I got involved, I realised the problems that existed with the job. The production was extremely low, and the relations between my company and the main contractor and the clerk of works and the checking engineer were the lowest that could exist. Some of the piles were being condemned and they had to be replaced, which cost a lot of money for the company. I was put in the job in effect in third position, so I had nothing to do with the running of the job. One morning, a pile was condemned because it was not vertical; the foreman in charge phoned the office, and the job director, Mr Frank, and a supervisor and the contract engineer arrived to try to sort things out.

Mr Frank went to see the clerk of works to see if he could smooth things out. In fact, the clerk of works told him to get out of his office because he was making it dirty.

Mr Adams was discussing it with the job engineer site foreman and the supervisor, and he called me and asked me why the machine driver kept digging if the hole was not going vertical. Because I always called a spade a spade, I told him the foreman knew. He phoned the engineer, and the engineer from 30 miles away told him to carry on and you ask me why the driver carried on. I could see Mr Frank's face changing with anger and he said, 'Charlie is right,' and I responded by saying, 'I know I am right.' Mr Adams told me not to rub it in. After a while, Mr Adams asked me if he put me in charge, could I improve the job. I suggested that he change the bonus so I had something to work on with the boys more than me being in charge. Mr Adams called all the drivers to have a chat with them and told them that I was going to be in charge, and it was welcomed by all of them. One of them commented that I should be made a supervisor.

Mr Adams told me he increased the bonus, and I was in charge next morning, and he hoped that I would improve by next Wednesday because he had a meeting and he'd be in trouble if things didn't improve. I told him to get rid of the foreman because I didn't want him. He asked me how I was going to manage. I said, 'I will manage.'

It was time to go home, and I started to realise what happened in that few hours. Here I was from six piles to sixteen hundred piles and eight rings. I never had more than two rings, and all the problems with all the site personnel, at least I learned that I was welcomed by our labour force which amounted to about 40.

So, I made some plans for next morning. I started by having a word with one of the men I trusted and asked him if he'd like to be my assistant, and after I told him the pay and conditions, he accepted. Then I had a word with the rest of the team and explained the way things were going to change and how the work was to be carried out.

I had a word with the guy that used to make the tea and asked him if he'd do the writing for me. He accepted and was very pleased to do it because his wages increased by a third because he was on miserable wages, so I got my team together.

The next thing I had to do was introduce myself to the site management. Because Mr Adams could not face them, I had to do it myself that morning, so I went to the clerk of works and I was wondering what sort of reception I was going to get, but as usual I was prepared to face what was to come my way. I went in, introduced myself, and told him that from this morning I was taking over the job and that I had got rid of all the previous people and everything was going to change. I would make sure that all the casing was put in vertical, but below that, I couldn't guarantee that the piles would be perfect. He replied, 'I am not Jesus Christ and I am not perfect either,' and I realised that things could be better.

Then I went to the site manager and the resident engineer, and I got a very good reception because they were pleased to get rid of the previous regime.

I left their offices and thought I would take stock of how things were progressing, and I began to realise the task I was facing. The job was a lot bigger than I had ever done, spread on a hillside over half a mile long, and the cooperation between the job authorities and my company was zero.

I went to see my understudy Bob to see if he was happy with everything and that if he needed help, he only needed to ask and when a pile needed checking to let me know. Then I had a chat with some of the rig drivers and had a look at some of the piles to see if they were vertical. We had two machine drivers from Northern Ireland, so I had a chat with them because the pile that was condemned yesterday was one of theirs. I told them if they needed any help, I was there to help. I looked down the piles to make sure I didn't have the same problem as yesterday. I checked all the materials to make sure I had enough for the day, and everything seemed to be all right so I went back to the office to check on the paperwork. Everything was up to date, and I looked at the production and it was between 30 and 39 a week, and one or two piles were being condemned every day, so I waited for the first piles to be checked to see what would happen. I looked to what plant I need, and I ordered some sharp cutting shoes urgently and the same amount for next week.

Bob told me the clerk of works, Mr Gold, was coming to check some piles, so I went out with him, and I could see Mr Gold and the resident engineer coming together, which was not good news because one is slow to make judgment first. They had a good look and passed all the piles, and they were pleased with what they'd seen, and I was happy because I thought we were on our way. The job started improving right away and relations improved, and no more piles were condemned, and Mr Adams was happy to go to his meeting. I was still worried that something could wrong. Two weeks passed and Mr Gold started having a cup of coffee with me when he come to my office. My management kept away and I managed the job completely with no interference from anybody. The original foreman was given a job as a supervisor to keep him away from the job when he finished with his father's funeral.

As the weeks went by, the production went sky-high because when I took over, it was about 39 a week, and we were doing between 90 and 100 a week, unfortunately never quite a hundred. After a few weeks, Mr Adams came on site and when he walked in my office, he greeted me, 'Hello, Charles. Have a cigar.' While he was in my office, Mr Gold walked in, looked at Mr Adams and told me he'd see me later.

One morning, Mr Gold was in my office and I told him that I was having trouble with my car, and he suggested a spare part I should change so I did, and the problem was fixed.

Next morning, I told Mr Gold that I bought the part from a shop near the job and saved some money because I could buy things trade. He asked if I could buy a set of tyres for him. I said, 'I can do better than that, I will get you a set myself, tell me the size and Iwill see what I can do.'

I phoned Mr Adams and told him that I promised Mr Gold a set of tyres and asked if he could arrange it. He asked how I arranged it and I said a chance happened and I took it, so he told me to leave it with him. The next morning a brand-new set of tyres arrived, and when I told him, Mr Gold was over the moon and after that became more cooperative.

One Friday morning, I arrived on site and all the huts except my office were burned to the ground. I went to our depot, which was in Mitcham, not far from the job, and I got 50 pairs of boots and 50 boiler suits. I asked the men to sign for them and some of the top hands signed OK, then a guy that started a few days before refused to sign, and before he finished, the others threw the clothes back. It was hard for me to believe what was happening, so I asked why they'd done it and they said because they wanted to buy their own clothes. I told them Friday was the best day for earning money but they wouldn't hear of it.

Eleven tons of cement arrived and I asked them to unload it, but nobody moved. As it happened, I had started four men that morning, so I asked the mixer driver to go and make sure to stack it properly because he was the one that had to use it. He got up but when I looked back, he was sitting down, and when I looked at him, he opened his arms as if he was told to sit down. I got the new starters to unload the cement.

I phoned the office and told them that the huts burned and asked for somebody to bring some money to the job. In the meantime, I ordered more accommodation, and it arrived that afternoon. The money arrived, and the men went and got some clothes to wear and went back to work. Late that afternoon, the neighbours started coming into my office, telling me that the gas explosion broke some glass in their windows, and as the days went by, they were coming from far away complaining and I just took their addresses and sent them away. A few days after, I sacked the man who started it all and good riddance.

The job came to an end and I walked away with a smile on my face, and when I got home, I got a letter that I was promoted to grade one foreman.

Because I had no job to go to, I sat home for a few days. One morning, Mr Adams phoned me and told me they had a problem on a job in Surrey pulling casing out of the ground for four days, and asked me to go and see if I could help.

Next morning I met the foreman, a very nice man, and we were very friendly. He made a cup of tea and we had a bit of banter and I told him I would pull the casing out in no time, and we discussed the job and the problem. Eight am arrived, and the rig crew and myself went to see what I could do. I had a look at the setup and it was OK, but because the casings were jammed in the rock, I changed the way they were pulling and instead, I decided to try to snatch them out. So we got all set, and I went to drive the machine, and as I looked the foreman was watching from a far distance away. Within five minutes, the casings were freed, so I signalled the foreman that the casing were up and he made a gesture with his hands that I couldn't explain.

I went to his office, had a chat, and I got away from the job as quick as I could, and I went straight home.

When I got home, I phoned the liaison officer and told him I had pulled the casing and now I was home. After an hour, he phoned me back and told me Mr Adams wanted me to go and have a look at a couple of jobs and report to him if I had anything to say. I asked him where I should go and he suggested a job in North London. So next morning, I went to the job and the foreman asked me what I was doing, and with a laugh, I said I am here for a cup of coffee. Before we finished, he received a message to phone the office, and when he came back he gave an address to go to a job in Winchmore Hill because the men were on strike and the office wanted me to go and sort it out.

When I got on site and talked to the men, the problem was that they'd been on the job two weeks and they had no bonus set. I promised them that I would get somebody out that day and if nobody came, they'd go on strike tomorrow, so they started to work. I went on the phone and told the contract manager the situation, and he promised me that he would be on the contract later that day and that I would take over the job and the foreman had to go to another job.

The day went well, and we finished a bit early. I was in the office writing and one of the guys came in with a worried look and told me Mr Phil and Mr Sands had arrived on site and should they pretend to be having their afternoon break. I told him to go home and leave it to me. Mr Phil and Mr Sands, the managers in charge of the job, came into my office and Mr Phil asked me why the men were finishing early. I told him the men had been treated like dirt and completely ignored so don't blame the men, and he cooled down and we sorted the job, and they went. Next morning, the men were happy with my arrangement and went to work, and the job was finished on time.

I went to do a big job in central London. I had five or six rigs and after a couple weeks, the company bought a rotary drilling machine and put on my job to try it, but with a separate foreman who was Charlie's son, Brian. Charlie was over the moon with the new machine and his son in charge and kept digging at me, but I took no notice. Two days later my job finished for the day and we went home and left Charlie because he was on site all the time to finish the day. Next morning, I got on the job early as I always did because I liked to sort things out before the job started, and as soon as I put the kettle on, to my surprise, Mr Frank walked in my office. I asked him if he fell out of the bed to be so early, he did not look very happy, so I wondered what had happened.

He said, 'No. I did not fall out of bed, I came to see you. Last night I was having a drink with some of my friends and Charlie phoned me because they could not pull the casings out. I don't like to be disturbed at home with something that he was being paid for. I came to ask you to be a supervisor in the London area.'

With a laugh, I said, 'You must be joking. All the cockney foremen wouldn't like that and won't accept me as their supervisor.' But he meant it and told me to meet him in his office as soon as he got a replacement foreman to take over the job. He never spoke to Charlie and his son, so when he went, I told them what happened and Charlie was furious but Brian congratulated me.

Here I was, like the big job I took over, another big but different task I had to face being a foreigner and practically a new foreman – something that was not expected. Anyway, I would approach it with an open mind and see how things go and look forward to the job in hand.

CHAPTER 24

MOVING NEAR THE NEW M25: WOODSTOCK AVE

The children were doing well, Pat was coping well with four young children, Lisa lost all her bad habits and became a good girl, and I got a chance of promotion. The house that I was letting was going well, so it was time to try to think of getting a bigger house, and because if I got the promotion, I would be doing a lot of driving, it had to be near the new M25.

I started looking in Romford, and finally I found one near the M25, near schools, and I could extend it and make a four-bedroom house.

We moved in and found a good Catholic school for the children. The guy I bought the house from left holes where he had dug foundations for an extension he was going to build, so I filled them in and started sorting the garden. There was a wooden garage when we moved in, and I moved it to the garden to use as a shed and bought a greenhouse and some fruit trees and started to save some money to build the extension. I went to see Mr Frank about the supervisor job, and he told me that he was going to send a memo to all concerned about my new job and my pay while I was on trial, and to pick a car from the garage that was in the office yard. About my new job all he said was that it was my job, do it as I think, and if I had something to say, just say it, and that I would report to Mr Adams, who had become an area manager by now.

Woodstock Ave as I bought it

When I finished

So I went to see him and we had a little chat, and he told me how he wanted me to do the job and to report to him every week, which I did not like. The jobs would be shared with Charlie, and we would have different jobs to control. Another thing I remember him saying was that the company would never have another supervisor with the power that George Bell had. I must say I was surprised to hear that after Mr Frank's chat to do the job as I saw fit. So I told Mr Adams, 'You must believe in ghosts because I don't see Mr Bell around, and we have something in common because I believe in ghosts as well.' Little did he know that my power would come from experience and respect, and especially from him.

With Charlie and me sharing the jobs, sometimes we met, and he kept telling me how much he was more senior than me and how he got more money than me. But I knew I was the new kid on the block and treated him with contempt until one morning the job he was in charge of in Carnaby Street did not have any men to unload the plant that had arrived on site. So to help the situation, I took two men in my car, and when they started unloading the plant, Charlie and the engineer in charge of the job arrived on site, and right away Charlie started asking why I was on the job because it was his job. After the third time, the engineer told him, 'You better go away because this is Charlie's job from now on and you are not allowed to be here.' He got in his car and went, and that was the first time that he finished being embarrassing.

On one of the jobs we had in the city, I had the problem the men on site were working slow because the money was no good. One night at about 10, the engineer phoned me and told me to go on site and take one of the machine drivers and replace him. I told him that I would not do it, and I went to the office and discussed it with Mr Adams. Mr Adams agreed that I should go and discuss it on site and make my own decision.

I went on site, got the boys together and explained the situation, and reminded them that it was not long since I was in the same situation that they were in. After a little chat, I gave them a little time to think it over and after a while, to my relief, they decided to go to work as normal.

I settled in the job, and I did not have the race or personal problems that I expected. Some of the foremen thought they should have been promoted themselves, but only one showed his anger, Billy Oldham. I went on his job, and he never talked to me as I walked on site. If he went to his office and I went in his office, he walked out. Because there was no need to talk to Bill, I completely ignored the situation until I had something to say.

In the middle of Upper Thames Street, as we were crossing the road, Mr Frank told me that that I had got the job and started to discuss my wages. He told me my salary would be £2,500 and I told him that was not enough, and he said he'd see what he could do. A few days after, I got Charlie's pay slip and I found out that I was offered more than him. Of course, when I told Mr Frank, he said I thought that would stop you arguing, but it was a mistake, and he increased my salary by £150 and all the conditions that come with the job. I accepted, and he said he would confirm it with a letter and a memo to everybody concerned.

Charlie carried on telling me how senior he was and started telling me that he was paid more than me again but I knew better.

Billy was in charge of a job in the City of London and the job developed a big problem. None of our doing as it was to do with an existing drain. So one morning, we had a meeting to see if we could resolve it, about 10 of us started to discuss it and after a while I got fed up and walked away, pretending to look at something else. Billy followed me and asked me what I thought because he'd rather hear what I had to say than those guys over there. So I told him what I thought, and he agreed with what I said and to go and tell the others. I told him, 'Let them sweat a little and they will learn a lesson.' So we went and they accepted my suggestion and we did it and it worked OK. From then on, Billy and I became friendly.

On Monday mornings, I used to go to the office and check the time sheets, and one of the things I used to check was the fares the men were getting from home to the job. On one of the jobs, I found that one guy was getting too much, so I asked Charlie to have a word with him. About 10 minutes later, the foreman came on the phone and asked me why I was asking about his fares.

I realised right away that Charlie had tried to stir things up with the foreman. I asked him why he travelled longer than the man in question, but the man was getting more fares than him. As he was dropping the phone, I heard him calling Charlie names, and I suppose he went to have a right go at Charlie.

After a while, Charlie retired and, unfortunately, he did not live a lot longer. I was asked to recommend one of the foremen as my assistant and to the surprise of a

My children

lot of the other foremen, I recommended Tom Oates. He was accepted, and I was pleased he was accepted because he was not tribal or racist and, like me, he was not ambitious.

We made a good team and worked well together, and were good friends for a long time until he retired. Unfortunately, he did not live much longer.

I started thinking about building an extension on the house, and a guy in the office did the drawings and I was ready to start. I started digging the foundations, and because the house next door was lower than mine, I had to go down about one and a half metres, and next to it there was a drain which I was worried about collapsing. I had a mixer and the materials ready and arranged for the inspector to come first thing in the morning. He arrived about 11 and I started concreting about 12. It started to rain, and eventually we had the biggest rainfall in the history of Romford. I went in from the rain, and when I went to have a look, I found the trench half full of water. As I said before about the drain and the depth of the trench and I had to go down with a bucket to get all the water out, I was very worried that I could get buried in it.

I tried to shore it up but I did not have enough timber, so I told Pat to stick around while I was in the trench. While I was struggling to get the water out and on the verge of crying because of the big problem I was facing, she started making a joke of it all, but I did not tell her what could happen because besides the water, some material also fell in the trench. I eventually got to some of the bottom and concreted as I cleared a length. About 6pm, I got a phone call from Julian, who asked if I needed any help, and I told him what a state I was in. He said he'd come over and bring Tom with him and they would leave right away.

I kept looking at my watch as time was going on and finally, to my relief, they arrived and started to work. My phone kept ringing and I told Pat not to answer it, but after a while British Telecom put a buzzer on and it was going all evening. All three of us worked very hard, and we finished about midnight, exhausted but happy because I had no accidents.

I started building up to the damp course and looking for a bricklayer. I found a 70-year-old who somebody recommended and he built most of it, but when he got a bit high one morning, he did not come, so I carried on and finished the building of the garage and bedroom. I put the roof on and got a guy to do the felt. By this time, the boys wanted to see upstairs, so I took them up the ladder to have a look at the new bedroom.

I opened a door from the main house into the new bedroom and got a plasterer to do the bedroom, so now I could start on the kitchen. I built the kitchen all by myself except the electrics and the felt on the roof. I used to suffer with a bad back, and when I was doing the floor, I finished it on my knees in concrete, but I carried on till I finished it.

Next, I built a big shed at the bottom of the garden to replace the garage I had put up before.

We bought some chickens for the eggs and some rabbits to breed and some birds to try to breed. Next, I built a lean-to, and now the house was finished.

Although I used to work long hours and had four kids to keep up with, I looked for something to do, so we got an allotment and Pat liked working in it. We got another one and another one, so that made three. We used to go Saturday or Sunday and the boys used to enjoy playing in horse manure. Pat and I went during

My Aviary full of birds

the week in the evening and we managed OK. We used to get a lot of crops and one year I got enough potatoes for the whole family for a whole year.

The boys joined the girls in the infants' school. I still had the house rented, the chickens and rabbits were doing OK, and everything was going very well, so I started to think about what was next. The boys were about six, so one evening while we were all sitting in the front room, I asked who wanted to go to Malta, and all the children got up, shouting, 'Yes, Dad!' Pat was keen to go so we booked to go in July, a few months away, for three weeks and we were looking forward to it.

The time arrived and we arranged to stay in my mother's house. Tom Oates was going to take us to the airport. The children told all the neighbours, and as we were leaving, they all came out to give as a good send-off.

We had a good flight, and my brother John picked us up and took us to my mother's house to a very good welcome. The boys kept running in and out into the yards until they settled down to kill as many flies as they could. Because my mother kept rabbits and chickens, there were a lot of flies around. John took me to collect a hire car and we were ready to start our holiday. The first destination was Mellieha Bay, and before you could say God bless you, we were all in the sea. Of course, none of them could swim, so the first thing I did was teach them to swim, which was easy because the sea is very buoyant, and they all learned in a couple of days and started to enjoy the sea.

When we got back to my mother's house, my mother and sisters were talking about a field we had in New Swieqi and that they were building next to it and they had pinched some of our ground. John had been trying to stop them but he could not, and that day was the last chance to stop them. So I asked them all about the situation, and they told me that tomorrow they were putting the damp course on and the land would be gone, and if John did what he had been doing again, he would be arrested.

At Mellieha Bay

Mgarr Harbour Gozo

I went to Malta to have a good holiday, but I could not let this go by, so as usual, I decided to do my bit. I told Pat what I was doing, and I didn't know when I would be back, and I got in the car and went to the field. As I arrived, they were still working, so I had a look around, went back to the car and as they were all watching, I opened the boot and just rested it down as if ready to open quickly, so they'd think I had some sort of weapon.

I asked who was in charge and told him that they had to go by me if they wanted to go on my land and sat on one of the walls.

One of the workers started walking towards me, but the foreman stopped him because he did not want any trouble. At that very moment, John and Rose's husband, Mikael, arrived. I asked the foreman to get in touch with the owner of the building and tell him to come because I wanted to talk to him now. He said he was in England, so I said, 'Get his representative in Malta now because I am not moving before I see him.' So now he started pleading that if I stopped them, the men would be out of work but I did not want to know about that, and again I told him to get who was paying him now because we were waiting. I sat on the wall, which was about a metre and a half high, and waited for somebody to arrive.

As I sat on the wall, I started thinking about the past and that I was finished with these sorts of problems, but for some reason, I started to enjoy it.

Going to the Blue Grotto

We did not have to wait long when this short man arrived, full of himself, and I looked forward to meeting him. He had a word with the foreman and came to talk to me. Standing below me, he started talking right away. I stopped him and told him if he didn't shut his mouth, I would put my sandal in it and push his teeth down his throat, so he shut up. I told him I wanted his address so I could stop the works before they did any more. He realised that I was not joking and gave us the address, and I told him to stop the works because he would pay for the problems that came his way.

To my surprise, he agreed, and I could carry on with my holiday, and when I got back to my mother and told them that we stopped them, I was a big hero with all of them.

John knew somebody and the next morning he got an injunction to stop the work.

Next morning, I went to see if they were working and the site was dead as a dodo, so we carried on to the beach, and it was up to them to make the first move because we got what we wanted.

After a few days, we were asked if we would go to a meeting with the owner to sort things out. We accepted and we went to the meeting and took our architect. The English owner was there, about nine of us sat around the table and the meeting started. The owner started talking stupid and John got up and started shouting. Because I used to attend lots of meetings in my work, I took the opportunity to tell everybody we were managing the meeting, and I told John to sit down because we were in charge and if somebody decided to talk stupid we would walk out because we were not in a hurry to solve the problem. The owner's architect suggested that he and our architect sorted things out. I said I wanted to hear what he had to say now. He suggested that because the ground was not square, he would square it up and share the area. I looked at our architect and he agreed to it, but we wanted to see the plans before the works could start, and me and John agreed to it and the meeting was finished.

I was glad that I could leave all that behind me and carry on to enjoy the rest of the holiday. By now everybody had learned to swim, and one day we used to go to the seaside and one day I took them to see different interesting sites. I was not one for eating out, although I used to buy snacks and drinks and ice cream and I went to the vegetable market to buy crates of fruit. When we were in Gozo, I bought a big sack full of melons to eat at my mother's and, of course, I used to buy crates of drinks.

Time came to go home after a good holiday and a good appearance for the children, who were all very suntanned. I was very happy that they all met my family and saw where I came from, which to them was another world. Back to the house, the allotment, and to work. By this time I was fed up with the chickens, so we got rid of them and turned where the chickens were into an aviary and bought some canaries and British birds to breed because I had birds in Malta and in my second house, so it was time to have them here as well. It was now the late 70s, and the children were doing well at school. We went to Malta nearly every year, the house was still rented, the allotments producing plenty of crops, and I was well established as a supervisor and became Mr Adams' right-hand man in carrying jobs and advice.

The company was doing very well and took over another department which had two jobs in London, so I visited the sites, one in Victoria Street in West London where the foreman did not show any respect towards me. I did not respond and left it to him. The other job was in the Highway in East London, and the foreman, Terry, made a cup of coffee and we had a friendly chat, and as it happens, we stayed friendly till a few days ago when his wife phoned me to tell me that he had passed away.

Next morning, I told Mr Mike Adams that I wanted the foreman at Victoria Street off the job before I went on site on Monday. He did not like the idea, and he was a bit worried who I was going to put in as a foreman, but when I told him who I was putting in, he was happy, and we told the manager in charge of the job to tell the foreman he wouldn't be needed on Monday.

Unfortunately after a few days, we hit a big problem in one of the piles. We found a well which was very deep. These wells were dug for water and were full of mud and difficult to dig. We had to use material to stabilise the hole, so I got the plant on site but I was not familiar with the mix, so I asked a friend of mine if he could help and he gave me the cold shoulder. So I got a man who was used to the material and got going and we dug the pile to the right depth, which was very deep, deeper than the well, and concreted and finished the pile and the job and we did very well.

A car I had

Another job I was involved in was in Victoria Street. It was a small site, and because of the restrictions on how to dig and the depth of one of the piles, it was not going to be easy to do the job. But because I was confident I could do it, I persuaded the management that I could and we put in a good price when we were doing the tender. We got the job at a good price. We got a date to start, and a lot of planning had to be done. I went to Great Yarmouth to see a great big tank that we needed which needed a police escort to get it to site.

The plant department had to modify the plant so we could produce the deep pile.

The day arrived and it was across the road in front of the Palace Theatre. The deepest pile was on the pavement and it was to a depth of 55 metres, the deepest pile ever drilled in London. I arranged for the plant to be delivered on a Saturday and all night because the site was small, we had to build the drilling machine in the road and the police would not close the road for two days. We constructed the deep pile on a weekend because the road had to be closed for safety reasons and the job was carried well by the foreman and the man, and everybody was over the moon because a difficult job was done with a good result.

Besides the day-to-day job, I loved a challenge, and one was on a job in Shaftsbury Avenue, near Piccadilly. Mike and myself went to a meeting before starting the job which we tendered using small machines, but while we were talking to the site management, I asked if I could have a word with Mike. We went on the pavement and I suggested that we do the job with a bigger machine which meant the machine had to be lifted into the site and make a load of profit. It was a difficult decision for him to make, and I could not keep up with him passing along the pavement. He agreed, and we went to discuss the idea with the site management, and I told them that we would be producing a lot more pile spoil and they had to clear it every day. But providing we could lift the machine on site, we would be finished weeks early and they could get to their work sooner.

Next morning, I met Derek, the man we used to do all the lifting for us, and he said he could do the lifting. We arranged a date and the job was started, and it finished about three weeks sooner than expected. A few weeks later, we were having our weekly meeting when the phone rang and Mike answered it. He did some listening and dropped the phone, looked at me and said, 'That was the man from Shaftsbury Avenue calling me a thief because we made a lot of money,' and laughing, he said, 'You are to blame.'

We used to have a Christmas dinner and dance, and I decided to start to do it myself. I spoke to one of the foremen, Tony, and he was all for it, but he wanted someone to help him, and he suggested Peter. So I agreed and had a word with Peter and he agreed, so I arranged a meeting with the manager of Tudor Lodge, a hall in East London.

We met one evening and had a drink in the hall and there was a show on. Because there was a lot of people sitting at tables, eating and drinking, I asked what was going on, and the manager, a woman, said we have a cock and hen party in. We never said a word when she said, 'You can stay, have a drink and watch the show.' We discussed what service we would get and agreed on the price and the date and stayed to see what was going to happen.

But before the show starts, I will tell you another episode in my job. Mike asked me to have lunch with him as he used to do when he wanted to tell me some secret or good or bad news, so I wondered what it was this time. He told me that the company had bought a piling company based in Croydon and he was in charge of it, and I was going to be made responsible for the bored piling, and I would be there in due course. He had a choice whether to stay in our office or move into the Croydon office. Without hesitation, I advised him to stay in head office where the action is, not in the desert.

He decided to stay put and two days later, it was official, and I was instructed to go and sort things out. Next morning, I went to Croydon to meet the manager in charge of bored piling. He was not very pleased to see me because I was there to interfere with his job, but it did not worry me. As I was talking, a guy walked in and asked me if I was Charlie Micallef, and I said yes, and he asked if I recognised him. I said I was sorry but I did not. He told me that he was one of my labourers at a job in the city when he was at university, and I remembered having two students working with me. He introduced himself and told me he was the chief estimator for the company. I sat down to discuss what I was there for with the manager, so he started by telling me how he wanted me to do the job. He did not know that I do things my way. Anyway, I let him carry on and he started giving me papers to fill out on a Monday and on a Tuesday, so I started putting them on top of each other till he finished. By the time he finished, I had about nine reports, which were neatly put together. I slid them towards him, and with a stern look, I said, 'I don't fill in any reports.' He looked at me and I think he realised that I was the one sent to sort things out and he put the papers where he got them from.

It was now my turn, so I asked him to see the labour list and it was a total mess. They had about 45 men and five foremen. I said I would look at them and let him know what I wanted done in a week. I asked him if had any jobs on, and he told me where the jobs were, and I said I would be visiting them in the week and I left.

During the week, I asked other areas if they needed any men, trying to find jobs for the men that I did not need, and after visiting the sites and discussing different things with the foreman of that company, I decided what was to be done.

I arranged a meeting with the manager to discuss the labour, and I told him that all I needed was six labourers and all the foremen except one, who was near retirement.

He looked at me and asked me what he was going to do with the rest of them. Because he tried to show me that he was the manager when we first met, I told him that he was the manager and to deal with it. He tried to persuade me to keep the foreman, that he was about to retire, but I would not budge and told him to talk to the personnel people in Maple Cross, our head office.

Going back to Tudor Lodge. While we waited for the show to start, we decided that I would take care of generating the money and they'd take care of selling the tickets. The band started to play, and a male stripper came out and started to strip, and when he got naked,

Receiving the 25-Year Service Award from
The Chairman, Mr Grundy

he went round the tables entertaining the girls. When
he finished, a young lady came out on stage and again
stripped naked and again went round the tables
entertaining the boys, so everybody was entertained,
and it carried on for about an hour and a half.

I started putting down names to invite because I
could claim money from the company for every name
that was going to the dance.

I invited all the men and retired people from the new
companies because I believed that new guys that joined
the company could see that we were good to be part of.

As the sale of the tickets went well, I invited the top
management to come. When I put in the request for the

money with all the names I was claiming for, it was all agreed.

Tony, Peter and myself met, and because we had more money than expected, we decided to do free drinks and get some shellfish because cockneys loved them and I liked them too, at the time, and I always had some when I went to the seaside.

The day arrived and we got there early. Eddy, one of our men, was getting the disco ready, and guests started arriving, and to my surprise, a retired man in a wheelchair from a new company came in, so I went to welcome him and told him I was happy to see him here because I believed in belonging. We looked at the buffet and it looked very good and plenty of it. To my surprise, the managing director, the chairman and Mr Adams arrived. Although we had a table prepared for them, I never expected them to come because the dance was for the men that worked on sites and sometimes there was an odd fight but, of course, everyone was invited. We discussed the trouble that happened before, and we were on the lookout for it to stop it before it started. Me, especially because there must be somebody to have a grudge about something and after a few beers try to have a go at me.

We finished eating and Eddy started the disco, and everybody was surprised how good a showman and disco man he was, and everybody got up and started to dance. At 10 o'clock, Peter and Tony got the shellfish on the table and everybody rushed to get some; it was a big surprise and very welcome.

Everybody was enjoying themselves, and few people thanked me for a very nice evening, including the chairman. I was chatting on the edge of the dance area when this guy stared at me from across the room, and all of a sudden started walking across the dance area towards me with a glass of beer in one hand. He was staring at me as if he had something on his mind. When he was about a metre and a half from me, I lifted my glass and said, 'Cheers, Mick.' That stopped him dead, and he sort of came to. He lifted his glass and said, 'Cheers. This is not the time,' and carried on talking. To my surprise, Peter was standing next to me; he must have seen Mick coming. It was really a good night. Eddy was in his glory entertaining his workmates and made it a good party night. Unfortunately, we heard that some people were filling bottles with drinks to take home, so we made sure they wouldn't do that again.

A few days afterwards, I got a letter from the chairman who thanked me for an exceptionally good evening. He and his wife had a very good evening and he hoped they'd be invited next year.

At home, the children were doing well at school, and by this time, I had an aviary full of nesting canaries and British birds, and they were exceptionally good to see after a hard day's work.

I will write about my life as a supervisor. By now, I was well established and respected for my experience, but it wasn't a bed of roses, as we will learn later.

Some Sundays, I used to cook the dinner, and because I did not cook very often, it was a big occasion. The first thing I did was go to the shed where I used to breed rabbits and took one to the garage, where I had hooks on the ceiling to skin it. When the boys were young, they used to have a go at killing the rabbit, but they were not strong enough to do any good and when they grew up they were too busy to help. Back to cooking. I used to enjoy the day and pretend to put all sorts of things in the gravy so the kids used to watch what I was cooking all the time in case I put something in they didn't like. When I made the dinner, I used to make sure that everything came from the garden, the meat, the vegetables, and for afters we used to have rhubarb and apple crumble.

And everybody enjoyed the meal.

As years went by and the children grew up and left home, I used to do dinner for all the family and sometimes a barbeque and it was nice to see them together. They liked reminiscing about the old days. I remember the first time I tried to do roast potatoes for one of the dinners; somebody suggested boiling the potatoes first before roasting, so I started to boil the potatoes with my girlfriend watching and when I opened the saucepan lid, all the potatoes were mashed up. You can imagine my face. My girlfriend ran away as I stared at the potatoes and I sprang into action by peeling some more potatoes to start again.

I made sure to have all sorts of meat and some Maltese food, and one that everybody liked was Maltese hobz biz-zejt, which means bread with oil, but it was the stuff that I put on the bread that they liked, and because it was a starter, I used to hide some for the latecomers otherwise it would be all gone by the time they arrived.

We also used to have bonfire nights and we had lots of fireworks because everybody would buy the ones they liked. When the grandchildren started arriving, the very young ones were scared of them, so the mothers used to take them to the back bedroom and watch from there. One day I had a party for Hannah's Holy Communion, that's her in the middle, and she had 15 friends coming and about 25 grownups. It was intended to be a barbeque but the weather had other ideas and it started to rain as soon as we came back from the church, so I had to get organised. The boys started to make up a long table in the kitchen so I could sit all the children, and the grownups would have to eat afterwards. While I started to cook the meat, luckily I had two cookers so everything was going to plan, the children sat and had their food and the grownups stayed in the front room and everything finished OK.

One Christmas, I had 22 coming, so where was I going to sit all the people? We could sit in the front room but I did not like the idea of clearing up afterwards, so I thought I would do it in the garage. I told my daughter Julie and she said it was not a good idea, so I asked why, and after a while she said it would be too cold. I said it wouldn't be cold, then she said, 'You've got all the tools and it won't be nice,' and I said, 'Nobody will see the tools, I am going to get rid of some of them and cover the rest with curtains, and you are in charge of the decorations.'

We started on the project and I put the heating on two days before so all the walls got heated. We prepared the table and 22 people could sit down nicely. I prepared all the food and as usual I had more food than we were going to eat; it was not easy to prepare food for 22 people but I loved the challenge, the worst bit was to get everything cooked at the same time. We sat for the meal and somebody said that the garage was too warm. The meal went very well and we all enjoyed it because everything was cooked to perfection. When we finished the meal, we went in the front room and forgot about the washing up.

I used to love the challenge of it all but unfortunately that was one of the last meals I remember.

The table ready in the garage

My Grandchildren

CHAPTER 25

MY TIME AS A SUPERVISOR

I will show the respect I had from different people I dealt with, and I will start with the men that worked on site. You may remember how Billy changed his attitude about me; we got a big job in Victoria Station in London, which meant we had to adopt all the plant to be able to do the job. I had a big part to put the plant together but because I changed a lot of the plant, Mr Frank asked the contract manager how something was going to work, he responded, 'If Charlie says it will work, I am sure will.' We arrived on site and everything worked perfectly and the job was going well, but one morning we had a breakdown, and the fitters got on the job and I went to see the problem. As I got in at the other end of the platform, and as I was walking down the platform, the men were passing me going to have their tea break, and one of them told me that the fitters

251

were blaming me. I told him not to worry and keep walking; another man told me again and a third man said the same, so I started laughing, and he swore at me and asked me what I was laughing at. They were saying it was Charlie's fault, so because everything worked well, I said I designed all the plant, and I don't mind if something went wrong. As it happened, it was not my fault because I designed the part, but somebody bought soft steel for the part, and when the steel was changed, we had no more problems.

Although the men knew I was their boss, they also saw me as one of them. The management – as I said before – the contract manager told Mr Frank how much he believed in me. Mr Adams thought the same of me because when he had a decision to make, something went wrong on site, or he wanted advice on a tender, he always looked for me. One example was when we had a job in Ramsgate. The foreman phoned him about a problem he had on site, so I was sent to investigate. The problem was that when the pile was concreted, after a little while the concrete shrank, so the level of the pile finished low and it was not good. I did not have any idea, but I arrived on site, had a chat with Brian the foreman, he explained what was happening and we did not come up with any answer. As it happened, a load of concrete arrived, so I watched the men fill the pile and as they finished, they put some concrete on a pile of chalk they had just bored, and I could see the concrete

shrinking and that was the answer. So I phoned Mr
Adams and told him what the problem was and his
answer was as us usual 'what a load of bull', but when
he dropped the phone, he went to see our expert in
ground material, and he totally agreed with what I said
and showed him a paper he had written a while back on
the subject.

One Friday I was on my way home and my mobile
rang. It was the managing director's secretary, who told
me Mr Phil wanted a word with me. He asked me if I was
busy at the weekend, and when I said I was not, he told
me that a piling company in Amsterdam which we had
done business with asked for help and could I go and see if
we could help. He asked if I could go Sunday for Monday
morning, so I suggested I go on Saturday so I could see a
bit of Amsterdam, and he said he'd get it arranged and the
secretary would be in touch later that night.

I arranged to be met by the site manager. He told me
to meet him at Schiphol Airport under the time, so I
looked for a sign showing the time, and the only thing
I saw was a big clock with this man standing under it. I
looked at his shoes and they were full of mud, so I asked
if he was the man I was supposed to meet and he was.
We went to the hotel he had booked for me to stay
overnight and the next morning we went to the job and
discussed how I could be of help. We agreed that if
Mr Phil agreed I could send a few men within a week.
I had a good weekend and went back to see Mr Philip.

We agreed he was getting the finances done and I got six men organised to report to him. I said that I would like to visit the boys every two weeks and he should put that in the price.

Everything was organised, and I went on a Sunday and met the boys on Monday at Schiphol Airport, got a train to Amsterdam, and got two taxis to go to the hotel. Although I told the other taxi to follow, he disappeared, and so I lost some of the boys. I contacted the boys through phoning the office and we got in touch. That evening, I took the boys to work because it was night shift and they settled OK, but after a couple of hours, the manager told me he had something to show me. We went into his office and he showed me his broken bookcase and said that my boys must have done it.

Of course, I knew that it was not my boys, but I kept my cool and looked around, and I saw the door into the site was about nine metres from his office and it was open. As I crossed Dan Square to go to the site, I was approached about four times to buy drugs. I told him that was where the thief came from, and it was a good job that I was there because if he had accused the boys, they would have walked away. He shut up after that and got on very well with the boys. When I visited the boys, they never discussed their nightlife with me because they did not want me to think they were enjoying themselves.

The job finished, and Mr Phil called in his office and told me that I was finished, and he was passing the papers to somebody else to sort the finances.

I did not have much to do with him, but after we retired we were in a get-together and he paid me two very nice compliments: one, he told me how good a machine driver I was by saying I could make the machine sing, his words. Another time as we walked along talking about old times, he told me how good the company was in our time. I said I was lucky to be able to do things my way, and he responded by saying it was not luck. By that, I understood that he meant they had full confidence in me.

Now I will say more about the companies that used to give us the work. We got a job near Liverpool Street Station in London called Broad Mews. It was part of a massive development that consisted of nine blocks, and we got the contract for the first one. While the job was progressing, they wanted us to try to construct a pile and cap in one go, which was different than we had done before, so we did a trial and I was involved in doing it. The site management asked us to go to America to see how they do it over there, so Mr Frank decided to go with the contract manager and the foreman but not me.

I was going to a job we had in Piccadilly Circus, and as I got near the job, a taxi stopped next to me and the client's representative at Broad Mews House got out. I waved to him and he put his hand up for me to wait. He told the taxi to wait and walked over to me and told me that they were not happy that I was not going to America and he would see me soon then got in the taxi and went. Nothing came of the American adventure and we were coming to the end of the job and negotiating the next blocks. I was visiting the job when I got a message to go and see the top manager a Mr Riches. He again said the same about America and asked his assistant Mr MacDonald to come into the office. Mr Riches told me he would like me to do the next blocks but he did not like the area manager, so we would not be getting the contract for any of the next blocks.

A couple years later, we had a meeting in Heathrow Airport to negotiate a job. Usually we started the talking with the lower management and when it was agreed, they called the top man to put the seal on the contract, but all he wanted to do was cut the price a bit more. They told us he was a very hard Scotsman, a Mr MacDonald, and I wondered if he was the same man as Broad Mews House.

We all expected this hard man to walk in, but as he walked in he looked at me as if he'd seen his best friend. He said, 'Hello Charlie, nice to see you again.' His team looked at me and wondered how he knew me. This used to happen quite often because I met some of these guys when they worked on site, so they knew me from years ago.

One day I went to a meeting with Mr Adams which was supposed to be very secret. We walked in this guy's posh office and sat down, and he looked at me then looked at Mr Adams as if to say, 'What is he doing here?' Mr Adams answered, 'Charlie is the nuts and bolts of the company.' So we settled in and carried on for about an hour and a half because it was a complicated job. I had a question to ask but I left to it to when they had finished, and I asked the question which they had not thought about. That took quite a long while for me to find a solution. I wanted to justify why Mr Adams took me with him, and the guy realised it as well because we got the job started, and one day I was visiting the job and he arrived in his big car and ignored his management on site and walked to have a chat with me.

Where the Virgin Mary lived in Turkey

Another job I was involved in, we were called to a meeting and it was unusual for the area manager, the chief estimator and me to attend such a meeting. We met the man and he told us the job was for a Japanese supermarket in Edgware in North London, and they wanted the piling contractor to construct the piling like they do in Japan. As we were discussing the method, I had a disagreement with the area manager because he forgot we were talking about something new, and the man agreed with me and realised that I understood what we were going to do. After that, he kept talking to me, and after a few days we had a meeting on site with everybody involved, including the Japanese, and everything went well. A couple of weeks went by and we were told that we might have the job and were called to a meeting. Before I went to that, I went to B&Q and got some things, went in my garage and made a rough template to show the workshops what template I wanted them to make.

Because we were leaving bolts on top of the pile so they would fit when they put the main steel frame up, the Japanese asked how I was going to guarantee that the bolts would be in the right place. So, I answered, 'We got your engineer and our engineer to agree the position, and I guarantee the bolts will be in that position when they put the frame up.' With that, my contract manager told the meeting about the template I had made and to my embarrassment, the Japanese asked to see it. So, I got it, and the Japanese were very interested and asked if they could send it to Japan. The thought that went through my mind was: *All the things they make in Japan, but they want to see something rough that I did in five minutes.*

We did the job and it went well and made a lot of money. When they were putting the frame up, I went to see how the bolts fitted and they looked very good. I asked the men who were putting the frame up and they told me it was the best one that they had done.

Mixing with different men, you learn a lot about people's behaviour, such as bullying. We had a bad job losing money and in a bad state in North London and the managing director, a Mr Ferguson, asked me to take him to the job, which was not normal. When I was discussing it with the area manager, he told me that if Mr Ferguson found me in the wrong, he would kick me all over the site. I responded by saying, 'If Mr Ferguson has a go at me, I will say, I did my bit by getting you here, and it is up to you to do something about it.' Now that was the difference between me and the area manager; he was prepared to be bullied and I was not. We went on site and he was not pleased with the main contractor who was preparing the ground. He asked me if Mr Frank had been to the site, and I said no. We went back to the office and Mr Ferguson told Mr Frank to get his ass off the chair and go and sort the job right away.

Another lesson I learned was that when there is a disaster, we hear how well people behaved. We were doing a big job called Chelsea Harbour right next to the Thames. We had a 25-metre-high machine weighing 60 tons tipping over. It was not a very nice site, and every time the driver tried to move, it sank a bit more because we had problems with the main contractor doing the working platform properly. I went to see the manager and told him the machine was going over and what was he going to do about it. He told me to try and get the problem sorted, and we would talk about it later.

Luckily, I had another big crane on site. I called the two drivers and told the crane driver to get the crane parallel with the machine and we would hook his crane onto the machine. He was to let me know when he was lifting 40 tons, and I would give the signal for both of them to reverse back together. The crane driver signalled me that he was ready, but the machine driver was still standing by his seat, so I told him to get ready and he never moved. I looked at him and he was frozen still, so at my top voice, I shouted, 'Micky, get that f****** machine out of there.' He sort of came to, got hold of the controls, and when he was ready, I gave the signal for both of them to go back, and we succeeded.

I think in a disaster, people freeze, that's why they behave that way. Another lesson I learned was about friendship. Mr Adams went to work in the Middle East, and Mr Ward became the area manager. He worked with the company in Brazil and with him came a supervisor. He was put to work in the Wales area. He was very friendly with one of the London foremen, and they used to get together with their families and go on holidays together. I went on holiday to Malta, and he replaced me while I was away, but from what I heard, he did not get on well with the foreman. One day I got a message to go and see the foreman and he told me to be on the lookout because Mr Worst was going to put me in the Welsh area and put the other supervisor in London. You've got to think before you trust your friends although it was in my favour this time.

A few days later, Mr Worst told me he would like to visit a few sites to see what I did for a living because he heard what was up. I took him to a job in Stevenage where the men were not happy with the money they were earning.

We arrived on site, and while he was talking to the foreman, I said to the men he was the new boss and to have a word with him when he was on his own. As he was walking, about 10 men surrounded him and started talking to him. I was watching it all from the office, and as soon as the men started talking, he started looking for me. I let him sweat for a while and casually walked out of the office. As soon as he saw me, he called over and told me to come back and sort things out because he had to get back to the office: Coward, and that was the last of his proposal.

We were asked to do a job at the south entrance of Blackwall Tunnel, and the job had to be perfect, so the area manager asked if I would do something that I had proposed a few months earlier if it would work. We agreed to do some trials. We got the plant and started, but things went wrong which could have resulted in a big accident. After that, while I was still shaken, the contract manager arrived on site, and because I was still in shock, I said to him that it was best to stop the project. He asked me to sit in his car and told me that he had full confidence in me and he was sure that I would be successful, so I agreed to carry on but make a few changes.

We had a meeting in our workshops in Doncaster with the plant director. When I finished with my proposal, he told me he could go to Italy and buy a machine similar to the one I was proposing for a quarter of a million pounds. I told him, 'You let me work it all out, and now you are telling us that you are going to buy one from Italy?' He assured us that he was not doing that and agreed to manufacture my machine. I worked with the designer and plant department and the machine was made. We started the job and everything worked perfectly, and as we were halfway, another job for the Docklands light railway came up and we wanted to use the same machine. We put the tender in and won the contract, finished the contract, and the machine went back to our yard.

I retired after that and the director bought the machine and it was put on a job near Baker Street in London, but after a few days, it was taken off the job because it was no good and it was then left to rot in the company's yard and never used again.

CHAPTER 26

MY TURBULENT YEARS

It was now the mid-eighties, the children were in their teens and doing well at school. I decided to sell the house that I rented but I kept the allotments. But unfortunately Pat did not feel well, and it became a bit hard for me to cope because I always wondered what I would find when I got up in the morning or when I got home from work. I was so bad that at one meeting I introduced myself as somebody else.

Pat was having treatment, but after a long while just before Christmas she left home again. It was a terrible period until I heard that she was OK.

After a little while, she asked for a divorce and I did not object. It cost me about £90,000 because to keep the house I had to borrow £45,000 at 15 per cent interest. I managed to keep the house because all the children were still living with me, but it was not easy. I paid Pat, and the marriage was over. The children were all working to help with the bills. I always looked forward, and I started going out some nights with friends.

Not long after, we had a recession in the country, and it affected our company very badly. One day, Mr Adams spent the day making people redundant, including 10 supervisors, so I wondered when my turn was coming. I did not hear that day but I was told to be in the office in the morning. In the morning, I met Mr Adams, who by now was a director, and Mr Oates the area manager. Mr Adams started explaining my new job, trying to make it sound good instead of a demotion. He was trying to make it a sort of sideways move. I was not happy with what he was saying, and I said, 'It's better to make me redundant like the others.' But Mr Oates cooled me down and I shut up and waited to see what was coming. I was keeping my position and the same conditions, but I would be in charge of big jobs, so I decided to wait and see what happened.

The company had an organisation, and I was effectively told to sit on my desk and not to speak unless I was spoken to. It was a terrible time. I think a memo was sent that told the staff not to talk to me. I used to be the first one in the office, followed by one of the managers, and when I said good morning and his name, he replied, 'Good morning, everybody.' But there was nobody else; it was as if he could not mention my name. This was after one morning a few weeks before when there was a traffic holdup on the way to the office, and 12 staff waited from 8.30am till 2pm so I could be present to start the meeting. Big change.

With the change, some of my responsibilities went to another two people, one that I had disputes with over a long time and the other was a woman manager. One night we went to a function in Doncaster and she made a pass at me, and because she was younger than me and very beautiful, I did not realise what she was after. I used to deal with her before and when I went in her office always closed the door, but after that night, I noticed that she left the door open. A few weeks later, I heard that she was having an affair with some other man and it all fitted together, so now I was in the hands of two enemies. The two kept telling me that I was a foreman, but I would not accept it because my title had not changed.

That time of my life was terrible with the divorce. Although everything at home was alright, at work things were very bad, nobody talking to me where before I was being asked for help and advice all the time. But as I had faced many griefs in my life, I took things as they came, and about three in the afternoon I used to leave and go home.

Management used to see me but I did not care because I already had two offers of a job. One day Mr Oates asked me to attend a meeting on site at 1pm. We attended the meeting and when it was finished at about 2.30, he asked me what I was doing. After I said

I was going home, the two guys that were with us looked at me as if I was mad, but my answer if he said anything would be that they made me redundant.

One day I was sent to start a big job in the City of London where we were doing something new with big piles, and that was their excuse, so I accepted. But, as soon as the job started, I asked for a foreman because I was going to leave in two days if a foreman did not come. The next day a foreman arrived and I put a man on to do the writing, so I just supervised as usual.

The job was going well, but one morning I was walking on site and I noticed that something was wrong when they were drilling. So I walked over to have a look, and I found that the drilling bit had broken and the men were trying to get it out of the hole. They could have caused a big problem that could cost up to a quarter of a million to put it right. I thought for a few minutes and gave some instructions, and while I was doing that, I got a message that my daughter was on the phone and it was urgent.

The message was that my mother was dying. Here I was with a big problem on the job and my mother was dying, and she would phone later. I went back to the issue, and we started to try to solve the problem again, then a message came that my mother had died. I told Julie my daughter to book a flight to Malta that night, and I went back to the problem and gave some instructions and we got the tool out without any damage. I told the boys about my mother and that I was going to Malta.

That night me and the children travelled to Malta because the funeral was the next day. There were a lot of people there because she was well known in San Gwann, and I met a lot of people and relatives that I had not seen for a long time. The funerals in Malta are very different because they recognise the soul more than the person.

Family grave in Hal Gharghur, Malta

San Gwann Parish Church where
my Mother had her Funeral Mass

I came back to the same job, and after a few days, a guy that had been with the company about 30 years was retiring. Because I used to organise a party for the men when they retired, the men looked at me to organise something, but I could not, and I did not want to tell the boys that the company did not give us any money. The best I could do was to take the boys to the nearest pub and buy them a couple of drinks from my own pocket. It was not long before the company needed my experience again, and the same manager that put me out to pasture phoned me and asked me to go to Heathrow Airport because we had a small problem, and he wanted me to go and see to it.

I got to Heathrow and it did not take me long to see that we had a very big problem, so I phoned the area manager and told him that we had a bigger problem than he thought. I explained what the problem was, and he told me he'd come right away. When we had a look at the problem, he realised what I meant and had a go at the men on site for giving him the wrong information. He asked me to go in the office for a quiet chat and asked me if he needed to write a letter to everybody concerned that I was back at my job. I told him I didn't want any letters because the men on site had more respect for me than the management.

He arranged a meeting with the main contractor and at the meeting we told them that we needed to cut some of the piles off using a percussive hammer. But because there was a big accident just outside the terminals where a tunnel collapsed, we could not use percussive drills. So we asked what else we could use and they told us to use jet water, something we had never heard of before. They also explained to us the consequences of us holding the job up because the machine digging the tunnel coming towards us cost £300,000 a day, and that is what it would cost us if we stopped it.

We looked for a company that did that sort of work, and because of the pressure we were under, I insisted that we employed a company with a lot of backup, not the cheapest.

We got the concrete cutting company in, and we started working round the clock, seven days a week. I was available at all times for the foreman to phone me when they needed me. As it happens, I even used some of the skills that I learned in Malta - cutting rocks in quarries. One day the foreman phoned and told me the concrete cutters were leaving. I told him to stop them and I would be there as soon as possible. When I got to the job, they already had some plant on the lorry. I told them that they were not finished and to carry on. I went to see the airport security and told them that nothing was to leave site without my permission. The men argued and told me that they were doing a job in Scotland, but when I told them about the security arrangements, they started unloading the lorry and started work again.

The job went well, and we did not hold the machine up, which was a great relief to everybody concerned, and I carried on with my job as a supervisor although it was not the same as before, because I was answerable to my two enemies.

Soon after, I felt very ill. My blood was very contaminated, and after I saw a liver specialist and a professor in tropical diseases and a lot of tests, they couldn't find what the cause of it was, so they treated me with antibiotics and very strong pain killers because I was in a lot of pain. For three months, I was going downhill, and I was getting very worried if I was ever going to get better. I wondered what the cause of it was, and sometimes I wondered if it was the stress I went through at Heathrow. After I was put on the most powerful tablets, I started to get better and eventually I was back at work but with some aftereffects.

After a few months, I booked in sick and I got a phone call from Mr Adams asking me if I wanted to go on long disability and to see the company doctor. I agreed and went to see the doctor, but he did not sign me off, so Mr Adams asked me to go and see the doctor again. I went to see the doctor, and I think he realised that the company were trying to use him to get rid of me, so he asked straight out if I wanted out. My answer was yes, so I was put on long sickness benefit, which I was happy with as a sort of early retirement.

I did not have to wait long to retire, and because it was near Christmas and the office were having their Christmas dinner and dance on a boat in the Thames, they used it to celebrate a couple of guys long service awards and my retirement day. Mr Oates gave a good speech about me, but a few minutes later, a couple of men that worked with me, one from London and one from Doncaster, told me that the way the company treated me was disgusting considering all the work I used to do, and I agreed with them because to us and Mr Adams, I held the company together, and they forgot all about it.

CHAPTER 27

MY RETIREMENT

I was talking to my son Francis about going to Egypt for a holiday, and he volunteered to carry my bags, so we booked and we went on a cruise on the Nile and three days in Cairo to see the pyramids and the museum. We enjoyed the cruise, especially the river and a village as it was a hundred years old and very primitive.

We made a lot of friends, and some nights we used to have a drink with couples Francis' age, and I was surprised how openly they talked about their sex life in very graphic details.

We saw a lot of temples, went to Cairo Museum and the pyramids, but the highlight of the holiday was when we flew over the Valley of the Kings in a hot air balloon. It was a lovely flight, very smooth and very good sightseeing to see all the temples from the air.

Me in Egypt the first time

Now it was time to start going out and starting to live again. Me and my friend Mick started going to dances where single people met, we also joined a singles club, and I started to enjoy myself.

The singles places were a sort of a cattle market as it used to be called, the old men chasing young women, and the women chasing younger men, which resulted in a lot of disappointed people when they were lonely. I

Dancing in Egypt

used to enjoy it all because by this time I was in a good frame of mind and sometimes I did meet women, but no one that I got on very well with. I remember I went with one of the women to her house, and we were getting on well on the settee when I went to the kitchen for a drop of water, and the kitchen was full of all the washing, as much as she could pile up to be done, so I went back and made some excuse and walked out.

One of the places we used to go to was in Newbury Park, East London. If a woman asked me for a dance and I did not like her, I had to find a way to get rid of her, so the next time we were dancing, I would say to her that I would buy her a drink if I had any money, and that was the last time she would ask me to dance.

The club we joined covered the southeast of England and they used to meet in Harlow, but they met where one of the members organised something like a barbecue or a party. We went to one of their meetings and we liked it, and we were invited to a party in Stevenage in a house that belonged to one of the women. It was a nice party and everybody was very friendly. I started talking to a woman and we got on very well, but she came from Cambridge and it was too far for me to travel. In the meantime, a woman started talking to me about Malta that she and her friend had just come back from and how much they enjoyed it. We found a quiet place and spent the rest of the night together. Her friend Rita seemed to be very attracted to me.

Next time we met for a barbecue and Rita was there with a friend who got on well with my friend Mick. I met another woman that lived not far from me, so we chatted together and they decided to call me Charles not Charlie. I don't remember who won, but anyway I made a date with the one that lived near me. I went to her flat and we got on very well, but all she talked about was having sex in the snow; anyway, I don't remember why but it did not last long.

We went to the next party to this big house. The drive was half a mile long and we met in the conservatory, which was the size of a tennis court, full of chairs and other furniture. I started wondering about the woman that held the party. She lived in the house with her husband, but they did not get on. Rita was there with her friend, and we all got on well together and made a date to meet in a few days' time.

I met Rita and got on very well. Next time, I went to her house in Bedford and went for a walk to a very nice area, and it was not long before she started talking very openly about sex, which surprised me. She told me what she liked and what she did not like, so it created a bit of a challenge for me to persuade her otherwise to the things that she did not like.

In America and Mexico

In Los Angeles

We had a very good relationship. One day, she told me she was going with a friend on holiday, so I booked a holiday with my friend Mick on a tour to the American West.

We booked a few days before the tour started, so we saw a bit of Los Angeles. We hired a car, and I did the driving, and we had a good tour around. One evening we went to McDonald's and when we sat down, we saw this place that had pole dancing, which we never heard of before, so we kept an eye on it to see what it was all about. A few minutes after we sat down, this beautiful girl sat on the next table. When she finished, she went into the pole dancing place, so I said to Mick we should go and see what it was. Although Mick was a great big guy, he was a bit of a coward, but he agreed and we went in. It was a big hall with a stage where the dancing was taking place, so we were looking where to sit and he insisted we sit at the back. So we sat on one of the back seats and watched the dancing, and the girl we saw in McDonald's got on the stage. So here she was in her birthday suit and suddenly Mick woke up. In one of the corners, a girl was doing private dancing. I said to Mick, 'I am going to see what it is all about,' because we hadn't seen anything like it before. So I went, and when I came back, I told Mick that it was his turn. It took a bit of persuasion before he said, 'I will only have the girl that we saw in McDonald's,' so he picked enough courage and went. When he came back, he had a big smile all over his face. It was time to go home and, on the way out he bought a picture of the girl, and when we went out of the door, he started dancing as if he had won the lottery.

We started the tour. There were people young and old and from seven countries, and an exceptional tour guide, and we all got on very well. Of course, there is always one, but we all ignored him. We did 3,000 miles and we visited a lot of interesting places like Disneyland,

Universal Studios, Sea World and Las Vegas and many more. I flew over the Grand Canyon in a helicopter, and over Hoover Dam and the Painted Desert in a small plane.

Me in Canada where I went Rafting

When in Washington, the guide as usual was exceptionally good; he picked visiting times when places were not busy so that allowed us more time to see more places of interest.

Because we enjoyed the tour, the following year we booked to go to the American South and follow where Kennedy was shot and where he was buried. So we flew to Texas San Antonio where I wanted to go to see the Alamo. We went to Dallas to see where Kennedy was shot, and I took a photo from the window that Oswald used to shoot Kennedy from.

From Dallas, we went Euston to the Space Centre, and after that we travelled through the belly of America, including New Orleans where we also went to pole dancing, but the girls were not to Los Angeles standard. I was amazed at the size of the cemeteries of the Civil War dead. We arrived in Washington and went to Arlington Cemetery to see Kennedy's grave, and I happened to see Audie Murphy's grave. He was a film star but he was buried there because he was the most decorated soldier in the Second World War.

We also went to a lot of interesting places, amongst them the Houses of Parliament. The people on this holiday were not very friendly and hardly spoke to us all the time and they were not friendly among themselves. But I saw what I went to see, and I was happy. I had a few good holidays with Rita, we went to Malta a few times and a tour to Italy. We went to Rome, Pompeii, the Amalfi Coast and many more places and a few holidays in England and Scotland, but unfortunately it came to an end.

Mick ran out of money, so I decided to go on singles holidays. I heard a lot about singles holidays, some not very complimentary, but I always had confidence in myself, so I booked to go on a tour to seven cities in Italy. On the way to Gatwick, I was talking to a guy who was going to America to get married. He asked if I hoped to meet somebody. I said no because I was going on the holiday to see Italy. I met the rest of the holiday guys in a VIP lounge in Gatwick. I was sitting on a chair when a woman came to introduce herself and told me that she'd seen my travelling label and we were going on the same holiday.

Trevi Fountain, Rome

On the plane sitting in front of me there was this beautiful woman talking to the next passenger as if she was going on our holiday, but she was too young because we were supposed to be over 50. She was in our group and her name was Charlotte, and she was sent from college to do some art. Everywhere we went, she was always drawing with three or four men walking around her. We got very friendly and she told me she liked to tease them. When we got to the hotel, we used to see who got in the swimming pool first. One hotel had mud baths, and while we were swimming, she told me she would like to have one but she needed to see a doctor. I told her I was a doctor and that night we were having dinner and Charlotte said about the mud baths and that I was a doctor. A woman who was sitting next to me, who I was friendly with, said, 'Charlie is a concrete doctor,' and that was the end of my doctor career.

Back to the woman in the VIP lounge. We sat for dinner and she sat next to me, and after we went for a drink, she was all forward about what we could do during the holiday and afterwards. She was not my type and I realised I must avoid her, so the next night I waited for her to sit and I sat somewhere else. She hounded and followed me everywhere for a few days before she left me alone.

I got on very well with everybody, but there is always one, and for some reason Betsy decided to start on me. One night, we were having dinner and she lit a cigarette, and this disabled guy told her not to smoke and she started on him. I told her that I agreed with him and she said that I insulted this very frail women on the coach. The woman next to me told her to 'shut up or I will deal with you' and that was the end of it.

A day or two later, after a long trip, we rushed to a café and the toilets, which were upstairs. Me and a couple of women came back from the toilets and I started queuing. I was served right away and got drinks for the women as well. Betsy was in the queue, and she walked out and sat on one of the tables. When I sat down, Betsy started asking me why I jumped the queue for some reason. I had bought a coffee and a Coke, so I offered her one of them but she refused, and that's how things went on.

Nobody liked her, so she got friendly with this very frail woman, and one night they were sitting at the next table and the frail woman came and asked me to give her a morning call. So I took her to reception and asked the reception man, he asked me what it had to do with me, so I gave him a bit of verbal. When we got back, Betsy had a go at her and asked her why she asked me not her, and the woman told her that she'd had enough of her and came and sat on our table and told me what a miserable time she'd had with her. Charlotte decided to go to bed, and I noticed her bag was still under the table, so I told the woman Mary sitting next to me and she said we should take it to reception. I said, 'We had better give it to Charlotte because when she gets up in the morning, she'll be desperate,' so Mary asked if anybody know were Charlotte's room was, and I said it was next to mine.

Everybody looked at me as if I had done something wrong. Mary picked the bag up, and when we knocked on Charlotte's door, I told her that she left her bag downstairs.

Towards the end of the holiday, we went to the shopping area on the train to Milan. I was going with this Brazilian woman, and the disabled man asked if he could come with us, so the three of us went. On the way back, an Italian woman told the Brazilian woman about this couple on the train who were going to pick pockets. They saw the disabled guy and the Brazilian told him to move. He did not, so she gave him a big shove and the pouch that he had on his belt in front of him was already open, so she saved all his possessions.

We flew back and said our goodbyes and went on our way, myself with very good memories of Italy and of a lot of friendly people. I enjoyed every minute of it, even dealing with the miserable woman because if you are in a good frame of mind, you can deal with everything, and I started thinking about the next singles holiday.

Next, I wanted to go and see Portugal, but I could not find a singles holiday, so after a lot of thought, I decided to go on a normal coach tour. The one I booked was from the top of Portugal to the bottom. I take

Venice

things as they come, and I tried to talk to some guy, and he responded, 'Me no speak English,' so as usual I took in my stride and walked away. A couple of minutes later the man came back and apologised and afterwards we had some conversation. He asked me to have dinner with them that evening, I accepted and the evening went well. He was a well-travelled man so we had plenty to talk about. Next day, he asked again, after I went for a drink and had a chat with another man and he invited to have dinner with him and his wife and told me that they did not get on very well. I told him that I was having dinner with another couple and if they agreed, they could join us and they did.

The next night, an Austrian woman joined us and we met every evening, we went to some interesting places, including the Fatima Shrine, and saw where they grow all the vines to make the port and the distillery. I also saw the trees the cork grows on. The holiday was very good. I learned that I could make friends wherever I was and I was worried for nothing.

I booked a singles tour going from Madrid all the way to Cádiz in the south of Spain. We landed in Madrid where we spent the weekend, so I took the opportunity to go and see a bullfight, and as it happened the best bullfighter was on, so I was lucky to see a very good ritual because it is very cruel to some people, but it is something the Spanish people grew up with.

Although the guide on the coach, a woman, was not very experienced, the crowd were very friendly, and because we were all singles we mixed very well, and some of us used to go for a drink at night.

We went to some interesting places on the way, and it was a different Spain than the seaside places. It was interesting to see some of the old villages. We made our way to the bottom of Spain into Cádiz, a seaport where England had a big victory against Spain. Before we got the plane, we went for some refreshments. Some of the girls asked for a cup of tea, and the man behind the counter pretended he did not know what they meant, so we all settled for iced tea. I saw the difference between the ordinary Spaniards that were very helpful, and

Having a drink with some of the guys
in one of the towns in Spain

the seaside people who see tourists as money they
can make.

I enjoyed my holidays, so I started looking for the
next one. My friend suggested we go to Spain, so we
went with Solos to a nice hotel and it was not far from
Barcelona.

So, one Sunday I went to see a bullfight, a very
colourful and old ritual, so I enjoyed it. We went to see
a lot of interesting places. In the hotel there was a
mother and her two daughters, who we got friendly
with and one day we met them near the Sagrada Família
in Barcelona. One of the girls asked me to do her

mother a favour and have a meal and a night with her, so I said only if I could do the same with her. I better stop there. The holiday came to an end, and we flew home with a lot of happy memories to remember.

I was on holiday in Malta when I met Rachel, a lovely woman we met during the day and spent some time together and arranged to meet that night outside her hotel. I arrived in the dark to meet her and saw this woman standing outside a hotel, well-dressed and I did not recognise her, so I stayed in the car. After a while, she walked over to me and I realised who she was. I took her to a hotel where we saw one of the best singers in Malta at the time, and we enjoyed it very much. She told me she was 50 and I told her I was 70, but it did not make any difference about our age, so we started a full relationship. We enjoyed the rest of the holiday. One night we went to a casino which she had never been to before, it was a country and western show night, and of course I had to have a go at roulette. After a while, I had a big win, and Rachel shouted a big scream and told me not to lose it again, so she put half of the chips in her bag and I lost the rest. We changed the chips and went home with a win.

We came back to England and she stayed with me because she lived in Leeds. Her children kept asking her to go back near them, so after a while, she went back to see them and came back. She tried to get a job down here but failed, but we went to Holland to see the bulb fields, which we enjoyed very much.

After a few months, her son got her a good job where he worked, and her children asking her to stay, so she had no choice but to stay in Leeds and that was the end of that affair.

I thought it was time to have another singles holiday, and after having a good look, I chose to go to Canada to the Rockies because I had heard so much about them. You could go on tour by coach or by train and I chose the coach tour. So I booked and off I went and looked forward to a very good holiday. The first morning while we were waiting to get on the coach, a woman started talking to me, told me her name was Janet and said that I had the same suitcase as hers. I thought it was a funny way to start a conversation. Later that morning we met again, and she asked me to have dinner with her that evening, which surprised me because she sounded very posh.

That afternoon we stopped for sightseeing and she told me that she lived in Lincolnshire on a big farm with 300 acres of land, and she had a business selling seed to the farmers. She got a friend and asked me to find another man to make a foursome and suggested a guy who happened to be a farmer. He did not go down very well, so the next day she asked me to have dinner with her again, and we had dinner every day after that, except for one night when I went with another three

FROM MALTA TO EAST LONDON

men to eat the local game. It was me, the farmer, a guy from Doncaster, and a guy called Reggie, a very rich man from Kent. It was a lovely meal until we came to pay the bill. Reggie, who was sitting next to me, suggested we share the bill and I said yes, so we told the waitress to split the bill in two. When the bill arrived, the Doncaster man said he wanted the bill split between the two of them again. When the bill came, he saw that there was a few cents more on his bill so he called the waitress and asked her to change the bills again. She grabbed the bill and screwed it up and got another bill with five cents less tax money. Reg and I went to have a drink afterwards like we used to do, and sometimes for no reason at all he used to start crying. One night I asked him why, and he said he just lost his wife.

Back to the holiday. We landed in Vancouver in western Canada, where we were picked up by the coach and went to see a very nice garden, and then we started on the way to the Rockies, which was miles away. The scenery was out of this world, and when we stopped for the toilet in the middle of nowhere, what a surprise! A cabin and a hole in the ground, and to my surprise, there were no flies. I think they could not survive in the bad smell that was in the shed.

The people on the trip, like every other single holiday, consisted of twenty women and five men, which included Reg the farmer, the guy from Doncaster, a big man that never spoke to anybody, and a weird man that the women did not like at all. The tour guide was good and kept us informed about the places we visited. I was glad I chose the coach because we could see the train below us going through the tunnels, and as the tour guide said, we could stop at many more places of interest. When we were in one of these places, a woman put her hands over my eyes from behind and said, 'Guess who?' I answered, 'No idea,' and she told me she was the woman from Brazil that we met in Italy, which was a pleasant surprise. Unfortunately, it was a brief encounter because she was going in a different direction.

One night we went on a visit to a nature reserve to see some beavers and the guide was following the trail of the beavers by their droppings, so all he talked about was beaver droppings. As I was coming out of the place, I met a few of the women and they asked me about the tour, and I answered, 'I am expert in beaver droppings now' and we had a good laugh about it.

We also went to a famous ski place; of course, it was summer, but we went on cable cars to the top where we had a very good view of the place. We arrived at the Rockies, and I went on a helicopter ride over the mountains. It was as good as going over the Grand Canyon in America and was an exotic sight to see the formation of the rocks. The tour was coming to an end and I made a lot of friends, especially Reggie, and we kept in touch after we came back to England.

Janet was booked to go to India in October and asked me to go with her but I was booked to go on holiday on that date. I did not arrange to meet her because she was too posh for me and lived too far away, although she wanted me to go for a ride on her quad bike to show me her sheep and land. I made a date with a woman from Birmingham, so I went to stay with Joe and he took me to pick her up, and she took me to see the nightlife in the city, and what a sight. As the night went on, she got very scared. We finished the meal, and I phoned Joe to pick me up and I got her a taxi. By this time, she was really scared of all the drunken men and women around and begged me not to leave her. Joe and the taxi arrived, so I made the next date and went home, and she said that she would never go back there again.

CHAPTER 28

THE THIRD AGE

I thought I would join a club close to where I lived to meet some new friends. I found one that seemed to suit me, so I phoned the organiser and he sent me a programme. If I liked one of the outings, I should phone the person who was organising it to arrange to meet them or come to one of their meetings because they met every month. I got the programme, and one of the outings was going to the dogs, so I chose to go to the dogs. I phoned Jilly and arranged to meet them in a pub by the dog track. When I got to the pub, I asked for Jilly and I introduced myself, and she told me to get a drink and come and sit at their table. So far, so good, but being a foreigner, always a foreigner, although I have been through it many times, it's always on my mind. As I was at the counter, I looked back to see who was there, and I saw this guy next to his girlfriend with his eyes focused on me, and I thought, *here comes trouble*. I got my drink and went to sit at Jill's table.

We settled in Romford dog track and the dogs came out, and everybody started talking about what dog to bet on, and then I realised that I picked the right evening. I talked to a few members, including, to my surprise, Steve who turned out to be a nice guy. Although I did not win, I enjoyed the evening and decided to join the club.

Next thing that was on the programme was the Christmas dinner and dance in a hotel in Brentwood. Francis dropped me, and as I was buying a drink I started talking to a woman and she asked me to sit at her table. I spent the whole evening at the same table, and it was a very nice evening and I met some more members. I attended some of the meetings and Steve asked me a couple of times if I had been on a cruise, and one night I asked him if he'd like to go on one. He asked if I had been before, and I told him about the cruise I went on with Rita to Spain. Because I did not know anything about cruising, we had booked a short cruise from Portsmouth to Bilbao in Spain. We got on the boat, which happened to be a ferry, and they took us to the cabin. What a shock; it was an inside cabin and we had bunk beds. Because I did not book the cheapest cabin, I thought that was the type of cabins they had, so I did not say anything.

Next morning after climbing up and down the bunk bed because I had a drink the night before, I said to Rita, I am not sleeping here again, so I went to reception and asked them if we could change the cabin, and they told me no chance. After a couple of hours, I told Rita that I was going to have another word. She got worried and told me not to have an argument. I went to the reception and asked to see the manager and they asked me which manager. I said the one in charge of the cabins, so she called on the loudspeaker and he arrived. I told him that it was my first trip on a boat and I was claustrophobic and if we paid more, could he give us a better cabin because I was not sleeping in that cabin anymore. He asked where I was going to sleep, and I said on one of the chairs in the reception room.

He looked at me and he must have realised that I was serious, he went to get a key and asked us to follow him and took us to a cabin. When he opened the door, what a difference! A big cabin, a double bed, and a big window to look out, and although he could see the expression on our faces, he asked if this would do.

I expressed my thanks and asked him where I paid the difference. To my surprise, he replied, 'Nothing.' I learned that you've got to believe in yourself before you can persuade others. We enjoyed the rest of the cruise and looked forward to the next one.

I asked Steve if he'd like to go on one, and he said yes, so I suggested he came to my house, I would get some brochures and we had discuss it. Steve came to my house and we looked at some destinations, and I asked him where he'd like to go because I was easy. He said

Acapulco Mexico

Gibraltar, so we chose one that went to Gibraltar and few other places.

It was a nice cruise; we went to a lot of interesting places and we both enjoyed it and we got on very well, and we are still very good friends. The club was going on a coach trip to Liverpool, and me and Roy decided to go, sharing a room. We enjoyed Liverpool and the other trips we had. Me and Roy got on exceptionally well, and when we went on a coach trip, we hung out together; we are still very good friends today.

At one of the club meetings, I was talking to Martin and we started talking about cruising, and he said he would like to go to the Caribbean. I said I would like to go through the Panama Canal, so we decided to combine the two together, so we booked to go. While we were waiting, I had my first knee operation and thank God everything went well, and it is still incredibly good to this day. When I was recovering, I made friends with Ann but because I had already booked the cruise, I went with Martin rather than with Ann.

Unfortunately, we boarded the plane in the evening, and we were travelling to Acapulco, which meant a fourteen-hour flight travelling in the dark. Because I am claustrophobic, it was terrible every time I looked out of the window and it was dark. We got to Acapulco where we spent a couple of days; it is a very nice place and interesting with lots of entertainment. We boarded the ship and headed for the Panama Canal. The day we were going through the canal, I got up at five in the morning and I got the best two seats for a very good view. Martin joined me with a cup of coffee and we waited for a little while as we approached the canal. I was happy that I got a very good seat; it was worth getting up early to see us going through the locks, it was out of this world, all the way through the canal. What an experience.

While we were at sea, I decided to give Ann a ring on my mobile, and after I finished I wondered how much that cost me. So I phoned my daughter Julie and asked her to find out how much it cost to phone from the ship, and the answer was about two pounds a minute. Good job I asked, so Ann used to phone me in the cabin and that was not very expensive.

Going through the Panama Canal

It was a two-week cruise, so we went to a few more places of interest like Barbados and Panama, where it was interesting to see the contrast between the rich and the poor; to see the way the poor lived in shanty villages and in squalor. I managed to buy a Panama hat, so I was happy. The cruise was over and we boarded the plane, and we had an incredibly good and shorter flight to get home. Me and Martin got on very well, and we still see each other at club meetings.

Because I had a flat in Malta, I asked Ann if she would like to go on holiday to Malta and she agreed to go. I hoped that she would like it because I had relations and a flat there. We got to Malta and she was very impressed with my flat. I hired a car and showed Ann around places of interest and a lot of prehistoric places and, of course, the sea, which is very clear, warm and inviting. To my surprise, she liked everything, the people, the food, Valletta, Mdina, and everything else, and she asked me if we could go again. I said yes, but there are a lot of places I would like to visit.

My friend Roy started going out with Janet, and her and Ann got on well, so we decided to go with the club to Germany. And although I had been to Germany before, it was a different place, I enjoyed it and we all got on very well, and we are still good friends today. It was time for me and Ann to go on another holiday, and we decided to go on a cruise, so we booked one going to the east of the Mediterranean. We went to Greece where we saw some prehistoric places such as where the Olympics started, Athens, and the Greek islands. The boat also went to two places in Turkey where we saw Roman ruins; they also took us to where the Virgin Mary used to live, it was a very interesting visit. We also went to Corfu where we had the biggest ice cream we had ever seen. I will not mention the price, but we enjoyed it. It was our first cruise together and we both enjoyed it, and on the flight back, we started talking about the next cruise.

After a few days of thinking about cruises, I always wanted to go to Petra in Jordan, so I suggested it to Ann. She had never heard of it, so I had a bit of persuading to do, but I was pleased because she agreed to go on a cruise that went to Jordan. So we booked and we were on the way to the Red Sea area. We landed in Egypt, and travelled to the port of El-Adabiya where we got on board the ship to sail to Addis Ababa in Jordan, where we got the coach to visit Petra. It was a long trip and Ann did not enjoy it because it was all desert and nothing to look at. While we were on the coach, the tour guide told us all about the people selling things and the beggars and hustlers and children we were going to come across and not to get involved with them.

When we got there, they put us on a horse to take us to the temple. It was very interesting as we were travelling through this narrow gap between the rocks. I noticed how they used to save the little rainwater they used to have. We got to the temple and we got inside, and it was just a big room. But when you stop to think how they cut it, especially the front into solid rock, it makes you wonder. We got out to see the burial area and it was massive. The whole place was magical, the size of it and the effort of it all, considering it was in the middle of the desert, and it was all worth it to come. Ann forgot what the guide told us and gave her packed lunch to the children. When the peddlers saw her, they tried to sell her some rubbish, and I had a job to get her away from them. It was time to get back, so this time we had to get a horse halfway and something else the other half, talk about milking it; anyway, we had to do it because Ann could not walk far.

We spent the night on the ship and the next day we had a free day. We got off the ship, and because we did not know what to do, we asked a taxi how much for two hours. We agreed the price and he took us to an old fort where Lawrence of Arabia fought. He asked if we wanted to go to an aquarium, but we did not like that because we wanted to see the place. He asked if we wanted to go to his house, which was not far. It was a big house and all the family were there including his parents and another couple. The driver took Ann to see the women, and one of them had a little baby, and I chatted to the father. It was not long before we got to men's talk, and he started talking about the girlfriends he had in the next village and asked me if I had any Viagra that I could sell him.

Petra Temple and burial grounds

Ann came back into the room, and she and the father started to smoke, so me and the driver went outside. I called Ann to come with us but she decided to stay, so I had to ask her to come because I could not leave her with that man alone. I asked the driver to take us back to the ship, and when he dropped us off, he wanted more money than we agreed, and he was unlucky because he did not get it. We went to some other places and we finished in Sharm el-Sheikh where we got an excursion to Cairo. Because I had been to Cairo before, I suggested to Ann not to go to the museum because it would be a lot of queuing. Instead, we went on a river cruise and lunch and visited the big mosque in Cairo and saw the pyramids. We enjoyed the trip very much, and when we got back on board and spoke to other people that went to the museum, they told us how difficult it was to get in and out of the museum with a lot of people crying.

We got on the plane, and although Ann did not like the Arabs and the desert, she enjoyed Petra and the other things that we saw, and it was an exceptionally good experience.

We discussed me moving in with Ann, but before I moved, I wanted to do some alterations to the house to turn the garage into a sitting room with a bedroom above and a bathroom, and the lean-to into a proper kitchen to be a self-contained flat. After a lot of problems with the building inspector, I finished the works and I applied for a permit to separate the house

Cruising on the Nile

Show on the Cruise. The horse was very good

and the flat, but I could not get planning permission, so I let the whole house and went to live with Ann.

We had another holiday in Malta because we used to have two or three holidays in Malta every year. This time Julie and her children and other people were in Malta, so we decided to have a day in Gozo. We hired a people carrier, and he took us to all the interesting sites. We enjoyed the day and had a good lunch and we got the boat back to Malta.

Me and Ann carried on with our holiday and we went to a Maltese evening. It was a barbeque in an old quarry called Maltese Heritage. On one of the walls there was a well like the one I dug in my mother's house, so I explained to Ann all about it. It was a sort of museum about quarries, so it was very interesting to have a look before we sat to eat. The food was excellent and the music got the crowd in a party mood, so after the folklore dancers, we had a couple of dances and at the end, it was a very lovely evening. In the morning we decided to book Qawra Palace Hotel for Christmas and the new year for two evenings.

In the meantime, we had a coach trip with the club, and after we came back, it was time to go to Malta for Christmas and new year. We had looked forward to it very much. We got to Malta and we went to the hotel; we got to the hall, which was very well laid out. The food was a buffet and everything was in it, Maltese food of every description and plenty of it. While we were having dinner, the band was playing soft music, after an hour we heard the sound of bagpipes, and eventually the band came in our hall and they played for a while. It was strange to hear the bagpipes in Malta.

Hollywood

The evening band played for a while and when it stopped we could hear a brass band playing, and after a while they came in our hall playing 'When the saints go marching in'. What a big surprise, lovely music. They played for a little while, and when they left the hall, a new band and a new entertainer took over the stage. They were very good, they got everybody on the floor, and Ann found a woman, and she was dancing with her all night, so she was happy and I was too. We enjoyed the music and the atmosphere. It was a wonderful evening and we were sorry it ended, but all good things come to an end. We booked Christmas and new year for the following year before we left for England with a lot to remember and talk about, especially the two nights we spent at the Qawra Palace Hotel.

After we came back, I started thinking about getting old and going up the stairs, so I suggested to Ann to get a bungalow together or build another room and a toilet downstairs in her house, but she was not interested, so I decided to sell the house and get a bungalow myself. I gave notice to the tenants and we agreed the date. When the day came before they left, I went to inspect the house to see if they'd done any damage. Unfortunately, they'd done a lot of damage to the bathroom, so I called the agent and told him to come over because I wanted some money before they left. He agreed with me, and after a big argument with the tenant, we agreed a sum, and the agent was going to stop it from the deposit they left originally.

The minute they left, I started to put in a new bathroom, and after a couple of days, a couple that lived up the road knocked and said that the people that left told them that I was selling the house and that they were interested in it because they wanted a granny flat. I let them in, and they were very impressed with my granny flat. They told me they were in the process of buying a house, but if we agreed the price they would buy this one. We agreed the price, I finished the bathroom, and they were ready to move in. I was alright because I was still living with Ann, so we started looking for a bungalow.

When I told people that I was 81 and wanted to find one that needed refurbishment, they told me that I was mad to think like that at my age. We looked at a few bungalows but I did not like the locations, so we did not look inside because I wanted one near a bus stop. One day Ann found one that fitted the bill with a bus stop a few metres away and also a corner shop very near. I arranged to view it, and a young lady showed us around. I found out that it was a shell, so I started to walk around again, and as I walked around, I said what I was going to do if I bought it. And I did exactly what I said when I had finished it.

I negotiated the price and I settled at a good price. Because it was winter and I had no heating, I stayed living with Ann and tried to get some help with the work. I knew a tiler who had done some work for me before, so I had a word with him and he recommended a plumber he knew. The plumber came to see me and he recommended a builder. I phoned the builder, Steve, and he came round and we discussed what he needed to do and when he would be able to start the works.

The bungalow as I bought it

As I said before, everyone I talked to and discussed the amount of work I had to do all repeated the same thing – that I was mad to get involved in such a big job. I got guys to work for me doing odd jobs, but they left when the work got a bit hard, but I managed to find other guys. My grandson Oliver came and gave me a hand in the school holidays, and he was very helpful.

The work was going well, the tradesmen were very good, and I made sure that I prepared everything for them, so they wouldn't waste any time.

The Chimney

The garden when I bought it

Foundation For Side Extension

When you are doing something, apart from the normal complications, you come up against problems you do not expect, such as the old storage heaters they used for heating, which I had to take apart where they stood because they were too heavy. To take the soil pipe to the new toilet, I had to break through five concrete walls, and one of them was particularly difficult because it was down a hole, and it had to go through the foundation and the concrete was 300mm thick. Even Steve did not have the answer, so I came up with an idea of how to get over the problem. Next morning I got up at 5am and started working on cutting the hole with a hammer drill. When Steve and his mate arrived at 8am, I told them jokingly that I was through. They jumped down the hole and they were amazed how well I had done because I was 200mm through, and I only had 100mm to go, which I was going to dig from the other side because it would be easier.

We had one disagreement in the beginning, but as I was paying, I wanted it to be done my way, but as the days went on and we got to know each other, we got on very well, and I learned that Steve was a good builder and a gentleman.

Me having a rest

As the work began, I started knocking down a big chimney that was in the bedroom; it was built of concrete and clinker and because the concrete was very hard and the clinker was softer, it was harder to break, and the dust it created was unbelievable. Because of all that, me and a helper used to do it in between other jobs.

Steve was working part time, so I had time to do a lot of work in between. One morning, I took the conservatory down because it was time to start on the back extension. Myself, Oliver and a helper started digging the foundations. The inspector passed the dig, and we concreted the foundations, next day I started to lay bricks, and I built up to the damp course, ready for Steve to build the extension because if I built all of it, it would take too long.

The electrician started, a man called Tony, who was a guy that I had used before. He had a big job because all the electrics had to be changed, but he got on with the job and worked well with the other tradesmen. Myself and six others spent different times knocking down the chimney stack, and when it was finished, I got it ready for the builder to start plastering the room.

Steve was ready to put the roof on the extension, and Francis my son, managed to get me the massive RSJ. I suggested to Steve to get some lifting gear to lift it into place, and although he was very hesitant, he eventually agreed, and I got the proper tool to do the job and how

The bungalow when finished

easy that made it. I think he learned something because I was used to doing all sorts of lifting.

It was time to start digging the foundations for the side extension. Myself, Oliver and a helper did the digging, the inspector passed it, and we concreted it ready to start laying the bricks up to damp course ready for Steve to do the building. Next, it was time to start the garden and the outside, and what a mess the garden was. I had to clear it, landscape it, and build a patio, the fence and a big shed. Steve did the patio and the fence, and I did the rest. All that was left to do was the drive, and Steve did a good job of it. He, like the other tradesmen, was finished, and it was left for me to finish the project, including a fishpond. Now it was time for me to move in, and I was very happy to live in a bungalow all on the same floor. The garden looked very nice, and because I had a big door in the lounge looking into the garden and the pond, I felt I was in the garden.

The stone that covered Jesus' grave

It was time to go on holiday, and we booked to go on a cruise to the Caribbean, but unfortunately I fell ill, and we had to cancel. Luckily, I got well and we booked to go to Malta for a month, and this time Roy and his girlfriend came with us as it was only for a week. I made sure they enjoyed it; I showed them around Malta and showed them some interesting places, and they were impressed with the churches. Unfortunately, the holiday ended too quickly and they had to fly back. Every time we went to Malta, we went on different months, so we saw different things that they do in Malta. This time we went at the end of June because they have a big traditional feast of everything to do with farming and folklore, so we went and enjoyed it very much.

As we did not have any holidays when I was doing the bungalow, we thought we would go on another cruise and this time we chose to go through the Suez Canal to see what it was like. We flew to Sharm el-Sheikh where we embarked on the ship.

We sailed through the Suez Canal, which was mostly desert on both sides, nothing to see, and we docked in Lebanon. We had a coach trip around the capital and some of the country.

On one stop, the guide asked me where I came from and when I told him I come from Malta, he told me we could be related because the people of Lebanon are Phoenicians, and in the old days they were great merchants and travelled all over the Mediterranean.

The highlight of the visit was going to two caves, one on top of the other. They were massive; the top one was dry and full of stalagmites, and the one underneath was full of water and we went round it on a boat. It was a marvel to see the two caves; we finished the visit, and I thought Lebanon was a beautiful country.

We got on the ship and started towards Israel and Palestine, which was the highlight of the cruise. We did not see much of Israel but we saw a lot of Palestine. We saw and learned a lot about the places where Jesus lived, prayed and died, and although some of them are modernised, like where Jesus carried the cross, you have to use your imagination. Sometimes you felt that you were in a holy place like the garden where Jesus prayed for the last time before Judas betrayed him.

Garden of Gethsemane and Wailing Wall

We finished the tour by going to the Wailing Wall; it was in a big square and full of people and lots of security, there were a lot of soldiers all over the square. It was interesting to see the Jews praying and sticking bits of paper in cracks in the wall like they had done for a long time.

We enjoyed the visit and now we headed for Cyprus. Unfortunately, we did not dock in an interesting place, so we did not see much, so we got on the ship and looked forward to going to Rhodes.

Rhodes is a beautiful island; we saw some old ruins, and we went on a coach trip round the island that was very interesting.

We headed for Turkey. We stopped in two ports and we went to some Roman ruins and a nature reserve. The Roman ruins were massive and there was a lot to see, and they were the best Roman ruins I had seen since Pompeii. We visited where the Virgin Mary lived in Turkey. We liked Turkey and we said we would go again, and we got the plane to go home and started thinking of another cruise.

We thought we would have a change from going to Malta; it had started to get cold in England, so we looked forward to a bit of warm weather. We booked a cruise that went round the Canary Islands, and we boarded from Tilbury, which is only half an hour away by car. The boarding was so easy and we sailed to Rotterdam, a very interesting place but very cold. From there, we sailed south towards Casablanca in Morocco, where we got a taxi, and he took us to see the sites and to a massive mosque and the day went very quickly. We got back on board and sailed south to Gran Canaria; the weather started to get warm and by the time we got to Gran Canaria, the weather was lovely. We went to a street market and a day tour of the island; we had a lovely stay and made our way to the ship. As we travelled north to Madeira, the weather started to get rough and cold, and because the sea was rough, it was hard to walk on the ship, especially for Ann, and that made her very unhappy. As we arrived near Madeira where we were supposed to be on New Year's Eve, because the weather was so bad we could not land, and we missed the fireworks show that was supposed to be the highlight of the cruise. Unfortunately, it was a disappointing night like Christmas Day, and because of the bad weather, it was too cold to use the deck. We sailed to Tilbury, and we put it down to experience.

In 2020, we booked to go to Malta, and we went from late February to the beginning of March. We saw some of the carnival, and people started talking about the new virus, so we were glad that we were going back home. Late March, and because of my age, 85, the doctor put me on lockdown. I could not leave my house, and up until November 2020, I had been in my house apart from just going out to do a bit of shopping.

My struggle in life was not over and in June 2021 I had some pain in my stomach. After a few tests with the GP, because I have private health I insisted on seeing a private specialist. Within a couple of days I went to see him and he suggested that I have some investigations and tests carried out. That was done a few days afterwards. Although he knew that things did not look very good, he did not tell me, although I got an inclination from the nurses that things did not look very good and one of the nurses insisted that when I go back to see him I had somebody with me. Obviously I knew what was coming. I went to see the specialist for the result and I did not take anybody with me but I recorded the conversation. He told me that I had cancer and that the sooner I had it removed, the better. I booked the London Clinic in Harley Street and when I saw the specialist he told me that he could do it the following week. While they were operating they found out that I was allergic to penicillin. I had a severe allergic reaction and for a few minutes was in a critical condition. As a result of this hiccup, the operation was taking so long that they had to put me in an induced coma. I was kept in the coma for two days. Things were not going very well but they managed to get over the problem and stabilise me.

I have been given the all clear and have been told that no further treatment will be needed. Thanks be to God, I am here today to tell my story!

Because I can't foresee the future, I have come to the end of my story. But of course, I intend to go on living a good life and having a few good times and good holidays and doing some cooking.

CPSIA information can be obtained
at www.ICGtesting.com
Printed in the USA
LVHW030607180222
711307LV00011B/1089